CW01217603

A LIFETIME IN THE CHURCH
AND THE UNIVERSITY

A Lifetime in the CHURCH and the UNIVERSITY

Anthony C. Thiselton

Anthony C. Thiselton

CASCADE *Books* • Eugene, Oregon

A LIFETIME IN THE CHURCH AND THE UNIVERSITY

Copyright © 2015 Anthony C. Thiselton. All rights reserved. Except for brief quotations in critical publications or reviews, no part of this book may be reproduced in any manner without prior written permission from the publisher. Write: Permissions, Wipf and Stock Publishers, 199 W. 8th Ave., Suite 3, Eugene, OR 97401.

Cascade Books
An Imprint of Wipf and Stock Publishers
199 W. 8th Ave., Suite 3
Eugene, OR 97401

www.wipfandstock.com

ISBN 13: 978-1-61097-540-7

Cataloging-in-Publication data:

Thiselton, Anthony C.

A lifetime in the church and the university / Anthony C. Thiselton.

viii + 114 p.; 23 cm—Includes bibliographical references and index.

ISBN 13: 978-1-61097-540-7

1. Thiselton, Anthony C. 2. Theologians—Great Britain—Biography. I. Title.

BX5199 T45 2015

Manufactured in the USA.

Contents

Preface vii

Chapter 1: 1937–60, From Birth to Ordination:
God's Repeated Providential Care | 1

Chapter 2: 1960–63, A South-East London Curacy | 14

Chapter 3: 1963–70, Academia and the Church in Bristol | 23

Chapter 4: 1970–85, University and Church
in Sheffield (and London) | 34

Chapter 5: 1975–2003, Contributions to, and
Recollections of, The Church of England Doctrine Commission | 48

Chapter 6: 1985–92, College and University
in Nottingham and Durham | 57

Chapter 7: 1992–2002, The Nottingham Chair
of Christian Theology | 69

Chapter 8: 1995–2010, Theological Contributions
to the General Synod | 82

Chapter 9: 2002–12, Chester University and
a Second Period at Nottingham University | 90

Epilogue: 2012–14 | 109

Preface

THESE RECOLLECTIONS OF A lifetime in the Church of England and in different universities give rise to a diverse series of anecdotes, which on the whole provide, first, some entertaining humour, second, a glimpse into both academic and church life, and third my attempted contributions to Christian theology. Teaching in five British universities, belonging to a range of Church of England national bodies (fifteen years on the General Synod, twenty-eight years serving on the Doctrine Commission, and many years on other Church committees), as well as such national bodies as the Human Fertilization and Embryology Authority and the Council for National Academic Awards, has left a reservoir of diverse memories that some have thought worth sharing.

At first, I firmly resisted the urging of friends to attempt an "autobiography." I had often regarded autobiographies as attention-seeking, if not tending towards megalomania. Yet friends pointed out that the combination of church life (both local and central) and varied academic experiences throughout the world might well provide a worthwhile story. So I attempted a first chapter. In the event I discovered that at the beginning there was more about the providence of God and my own mistakes than anything else. These chapters begin with a relatively high ratio of entertainment, but the book become increasingly theological in the later chapters.

Towards the end, my story concerns teaching in America, Korea, and elsewhere. Although the Church of England and home universities often provide the main focus, my overseas doctoral graduates assure me that the story would be of international interest. Those who have read one of my twenty books (and three more to come, if I am spared) may also have a special interest in it.

Anthony C. Thiselton,
June 2014

Chapter 1

1937–60

From Birth to Ordination: God's Repeated Providential Care

A LIFETIME OF PROVIDENCE might have been called seventy-seven years of miracles, in some circles. But the category of miracles too often seems to imply a "two-story" view of God's dealings with the world. For reasons that will be obvious, I prefer to use the term *the providence of God*.

The first act of providence was simply my birth. I was born nearly three months prematurely. My date of birth should have been September, rather than July, 1937. I gather that at the beginning my entry into the world was surrounded by an oxygen tent and anxious medical staff and parents. It was providential that I survived this, contrary to some expectations.

The second event of providence concerned my Grandmother's prayers from the earliest moment. I still have a poem, written in my Grandmother's hand, dated July 13, 1937, my date of birth. Of three verses the middle verse reads:

> Care for him, O our Father,
> His childhood guard from harm;
> And when he is in danger,
> Reach out Thy loving arm.
> Let thy wise counsel guide him
> Each step along life's ways;
> So let him love and serve Thee, and live unto Thy praise.

Kate Kevan also regularly prayed that I would be as Samuel, although I was unaware of this until Ordination had become certain. Both prayers were answered, as will be evident.

The third notable providential event, which many would call a miracle, came during the next two years. My Grandmother, Kate, and I both fell victim to the most serious and virulent type of meningitis. We shall never know who might have caught it from whom. But the outcome was that she died, while our general practitioner treated me on the kitchen table, then in hospital, and I was safely brought through the event. I never knew either of my grandfathers, and can probably only imagine the most shadowy supposed memories of my two grandmothers. My father's mother, Mercey, died in London in the Blitz; my mother's mother, Kate, died of meningitis.

Meanwhile a fourth providential event had already occurred. My parents had originally been brought up as Strict Baptists, but joined the Church of England because they regarded it being a more child-friendly church. God's providence concerned not only my future destiny at the heart of the Church of England, but also my parents' choice of godparents. Rather than selecting relatives, they approached a godly man and godly woman who were members of the local congregation, which they had joined, namely Christ Church, Woking. Both could help to bring me up within the nurture of the local church. I still possess the Bible given to me by my Godmother, and the Prayer Book, given by my Godfather. They also gave me a number of children's books of Bible stories and prayers. These bear testimony to their deep concern for my spiritual nurture as a child. I have kept these books of prayers for use each day, which, again, were imaginatively written and illustrated for children.

Although I began school at five years of age, it was within the first two years at school that I came to realize that I had a serious problem with my eyes. This would come to haunt me later on, but for the present my eye specialist recommended that, at seven, I should take a year away from school, and perhaps transfer to another school. Both of these were duly done, and I was able to begin at a new school, with a fresh start.

My eye specialist was a patient Irishman, whom I can still remember testing me as a small child with various lenses. He would repeatedly ask in his strong Irish accent, "Better or worse?" Even a child under seven could understand how to respond to such direct questions. It was afterwards that I gradually learnt that my two problems were, first, the more routine one of Astigmatism, and second, the more serious problem Nystagmus.

Nystagmus causes constant movements of the head and eyes, and makes focus on the centre of an object of vision more than difficult. This double problem made a prescription for lenses difficult, and I was providentially blessed that at the time my particular eye specialist knew how to cope with this. It would be different later in life.

Later, when I was in the Cadet Corps at City of London School, my sight caused great merriment on the rifle range. In the miniature range I unintentionally shot through the wire that joined everyone's targets together, making them all suddenly disappear from view without apparent reason. Then, on the full-size open-air range, I had the distinction of enabling my next door neighbour to find a six-bullet-score on his target, rather than that duly expected from the standard five bullets.

Meanwhile, at the age of seven I underwent more surgery. I had always been a sickly child. I picked up every possible childhood illness, from rasping whooping cough to measles, bronchitis, chickenpox, and the rest. This had been partly because my parents were fearful of exposing me to injections against infections. Looking back, I suspect that our house was probably damp, and in those days not many in Surrey had central heating.

The hospital or nursing home decided to remove my tonsils. I came through this safely, and then experienced a noticeable improvement in health. I was taken to the sea to convalesce, and still retain vivid memories of enjoying the beach and sea at Eastbourne. Since this was wartime, it was only my second visit to the coast. The only two beaches that I knew (Eastbourne and Sidmouth) were strewn with barriers of barbed wire and solid metal defences against the possible landing enemy troops.

I enjoyed most of my time at City of London School, except for the problem of my eyesight. I remember well the horror (as it seemed) of trying to master the Greek alphabet and Greek vocabulary, with Greek letters constantly swimming around. But eventually I caught up, and there was plenty to enjoy. The cadet core was not meant to be a source of amusement, but I remember a string of entertaining incidents. Not all were pre-planned. My size-nine boots appeared to look huge, at the age of fourteen. I genuinely misheard my Latin master when he asked, "Thiselton, are those seven-league boots?" Thinking that he had said "Size-seven boots," I innocently replied, "No, Sir, nine"—to the merriment of the class. On another occasion, an innocent boy asked the regimental sergeant major about choices of colours for boots. His incredulous, indignant, cockney, old-soldier, response: "*What! Brun Boots in the Army!?!*"

had to be heard for its high degree of shocked indignation to be fully appreciated.

Less accidental was my experience when I reached the dizzy heights of becoming a non-commissioned officer. Finding it difficult to take much of it too seriously, I found that I could get away with giving highly exaggerated movements and commands. I could swing my arms exceptionally high when marching. More to the point, the command, "Attention" could easily be transposed into "Attenn . . . *hp*, while, "Platoon, left wheel" could readily become "Läiift [wait for it] *wh*." The problem of poor eyesight was mitigated by the sad death of our deeply-respected King George VI. All officers wore black arm bands, which made recognition of officers easy, without the need to stare to see crowns or pips. This helped me to sail through "Cert. A."

For me personally, like many people, my teenage years were also marked by two tragedies. First, my parents separated, and I and my mother had to leave our splendid house in Surrey for a very modest flat in Wandsworth, London. I had soon discovered that blemishes could mar the lives of Christians, although this was none of my mother's doing. Second, in the Sixth Form, my eyesight seemed to collapse, and my eye specialist recommended that I should study for "A" levels at home. In spite of this, I went on to pass my A levels and to study for, and receive, my university BD degree.

After I had left school, and had almost reached the end of study for my London University BD, I went before a Church Selection Board, which would advise the bishops whether to accept me for training for the Ministry. The then bishop of Southwark, Bishop Bertram Simpson, who had been bishop since 1942, offered his congratulations because the Selection Board (then called CACTM) had given me an "A" grade in every section. But then the bishop dropped a bombshell. They had sent me to Harley Street, where the highest medical specialists practised. "But I am afraid you have failed your medical," the bishop said. I was devastated, and asked in puzzlement, "On what ground?" "Well," said the bishop, "*The specialist says that you will never be able to read enough books to exercise a useful parish ministry.*" "But," I protested, "I have passed exams in Hebrew and Greek, and read virtually everything required for the BD." The bishop asked me to list some of the books that I had read. I did so, although I also had to admit that I usually used a magnifying glass for Hebrew vowels. After a moment, the bishop continued: "This is quite ridiculous! I shall tear this report up, and no one will ever see it!"

This was providence indeed. My whole future, not to mention my sense of God's call, had hung in the balance. Nowadays people are frequently given second chances, but they were not encouraged then. The Church of England also makes most decisions by committee, and I cannot imagine a bishop secretly suppressing a report today. For me, God's providence, if not this time sheer miracle, was certainly in evidence on that fateful day.

These were not the only examples of providential care before graduation and ordination. I had several amazing deliverances as a boy on my bicycle. Of two outstanding ones, one was from a situation that was entirely my own fault, and one was not. We had few hills around Woking, my home town, and I had been given a speedometer for Christmas. I can't remember what year it was, although I was certainly under thirteen. In Surrey Newlands Corner was a well-known hill. I managed to cycle to the top with difficulty, but then decided with utter foolishness to see how fast I could free-wheel down the hill. At forty miles per hour the bike began to get out of control, and I sent up feverish panicky prayers. God kept me safe, and I am alive (perhaps just) to tell the tale.

The other took place later in London. I was cycling along Trinity Road, Wandsworth Common, South-West London, when I encountered a lorry or truck bearing down upon me directly in my lane in this busy road. I could see only that it was overtaking a bus, leaving me no room to go anywhere, except to make an abrupt halt, jump onto the pavement or sidewalk, and pull my bike out of the way onto the path. I was trembling with shock and relief, when a groundsman from the adjacent tennis courts rushed up to me, and indignantly exclaimed, "A driver like that is a menace on the road; he should never be allowed to get away with it! He is very lucky that you were not killed!"

Had I had time to think, I may have resisted the groundsman's proposal, but he felt so indignant and passionate at this near loss of life, that he reported the event to the police. In due course, I was duly called as a witness in court, and the magistrate pronounced in favour of the prosecution, with some strong words. I had to regard this as one more of many acts of God's protection and providential care. My Grandmother's prayer had been answered again.

God's further providential care was shown in the face of some long periods of pneumonia. The first occurred when I had just begun to attend City of London School. Travelling to school each day involved the delight of catching the 7:53 a.m. steam train every morning from Woking to London, Waterloo, and returning every late afternoon, often on the 5 p.m. It was a delight for me then to travel with London commuters, especially since City of London School required a commuter-type school uniform of black jacket and black striped trousers.

A problem arose at the School during one daytime. I felt extremely unwell, and was taken to a self-styled medic, called "Doc," to diagnose the problem. He took my temperature, and advised my immediately going home to bed. Whether he realized that this meant at least twenty minutes on the underground with a change of trains at Charing Cross, followed by a thirty-minute train ride from Waterloo, and a ten-minute walk home, I never knew. At all events I remember shivering ceaselessly on Waterloo Station while I waited for the next train, and arriving home trembling and shivering to go to bed.

In the event our doctor diagnosed severe pneumonia. My temperature reached around 105°; I became delirious; and had more than three months in bed. But God brought me through this crisis. Our clergy must have been particularly dedicated, for I remember our curate playing chess with me, when I became well enough, for what must have been a long time out of his precious schedule. I had always thought him a little over-solemn, until he advised that the only way to avoid losing would be to knock the board over, and then express contrite regret. The downside from the illness was that over the next two or three years I suffered pneumonia at least twice again, so was always trying to catch up what I had missed at school.

The trains between Woking and London/Waterloo were normally a delight. Often, especially on homeward runs, the steam train (for Basingstoke and Winchester) would be travelling beside an electric train (for Guildford and Portsmouth) on the next track. A "race" would ensue. The electric train always began faster; the steam train usually thundered through Walton or Weybridge, to arrive first at Woking. It was a schoolboy's dream.

On the outward journey to London, I often travelled on the 7:53 with my school-friend Michael Jones and his father. Mr. Jones loved radio circuitry. He taught me how to build my first crystal set, and then I slowly graduated towards ever more complicated radios, often built with up to six or seven valves. One could pick up numerous ex-army and ex-air force bargains from shops in Lisle Street and Little Newport Street, near Leicester Square. I bought some microphones, and learned from a book recommended by Mr. Jones how to build a transmitter. I had no idea that everyone needed to be licensed by the Post Office and trained before they could operate a transmitter. Hence my parents suffered consternation, and I their wrath, when my voice unexpectedly broke into their radio programme asking, "Are you receiving me? Are you receiving me?" But Mr. Jones had suggested a teenage hobby, which I kept up until dreaded miniaturization meant that my eyesight could no longer cope with components and soldering joints.

Several examples of God's providential care sometimes included saving me from my own folly. I remember climbing rocks far above the reasonable or sensible height, with few footholds, and becoming frightened by the fact that there seemed to be no easy way down again. Clearly I had exceeded what was wise for a child. Another example was my desire to undertake experiments in chemistry, when I had had no training at all in the subject. Naturally, when I sought to apply a flame to what zinc and hydrochloric acid could produce through glass pipes, although I got away with a number of successful experiments, eventually the whole glass container and tubing blew up, narrowly missing my face by fractions of an inch. God brought me through dangers of my own making. There is no clear answer to how much freedom parents should give to a child.

My Uncle, Dr. Ernest Kevan, was principal of what was then called London Bible College, later to be called the London School of Theology. I occasionally accompanied him on preaching visits. I especially recall a sermon delivered at Spurgeon's Tabernacle, Elephant and Castle, London, that particularly enthralled me. It was on the theme of the grace of God. When I expressed interest in the sermon, he simply replied, "That was pure theology!" If this was theology, it was certainly for me.

In the classical sixth form, when again my eyesight broke down, I found stretches of Greek and Latin text quite a strain, especially with the need to look up words frequently in a Greek lexicon and Latin dictionary. My eye specialist recommended that I should leave school for a year, and either postpone my "A" levels for a year, or else take them from home. I still have in my possession a certificate stating that I would never be able to be considered for a university course.

In the event, it proved possible to take A levels that year, and to commence the London University BD from theological college. Eventually I was able to benefit from lectures both at King's College, University of London, and from theological college. Although I identified with the more conservative stance of the theological college, I could not help comparing the relaxed humour with which biblical subjects were taught at

King's College with the more defensive and earnest stance at theological college. I could partly resonate later with Schleiermacher's experiences of Barby and Halle!

Theological college gave us experience of mission. On one occasion we were sent to St. Nicholas Deptford, a dockland parish in the East End of London, after it had benefited from needed internal renovations. One theme, taken up by the congregation, was "A new inside." One earnest Sunday school teacher spoke from Ezekiel 36:26 about how God would remove the heart of stone in exchange for a heart of flesh. On Good Friday a generous donor had provided the gift of hot-cross buns for the children. One child refused the offer because he had confused "the heart of stone" and "the new heart" of Jeremiah 31 and Ezekiel 36 with the hot-cross buns. He declined to eat one on the ground that "The hot cross bun has a stone in it." It was an early lesson on communication.

I also discovered the potentially huge volume of the East End dockers' voices. As we visited the new street, someone cried at maximum decibels, "Good Froidai! What does it mean to *yooo*?" The same person selected a "gospel" text on grace from Isaiah 55:1 (AV/KJB), and cried out at full volume: "'E that 'ath no money, come, buy woine and miook without money and without proice"; but as he reflected that street traders also advertised in that street, he mumbled, "Oh, I do feeoo a fool."

King's College was a delight. I remember a fellow student asking Dr. Ulrich Simon what a *Festschrift* was. He replied in his typically heavy Germanic accent, "Ven you are an olt man, and are no longer interested in your zubject, zey present you with zis book of essays about zings concerning vich you no longer vish to know." Sometimes Ninian Smart and regularly Eric Mascall received loud applause at the end of their lectures.

My Anglican college, Oak Hill, Southgate, North London, provided delightful years of training for the Ministry. The principal, L. F. E. Wilkinson, was a humble, generous, and lovable man, and was Christ-like in both word and deed. Typically he had above his mantelpiece the motto, "I can do all things through Christ who strengthens me"; and he had added in his own hand, "Very well then, get on and do it!"

THE COLLEGE FROM THE AIR

Oak Hill Theological College, 1958–60

The principal was frequently absent-minded, and often forgot our sixty-five names. But he had clearly developed a technique for dealing with this. His prayers for his students were particularly memorable. The principal and the student would flop down on our knees in his study, while he prayed, "Lord, we pray that Thou wilt be with . . . um . . . er . . . *Thy servant*, as he visits this parish . . . ."

Principal Wilkinson also had a wonderful sense of humour. His birthday fell on All Saints Day, and each year was duly celebrated by all the students with entertaining speeches, processions, applause, motorbike escorts, a birthday cake, and all the trimmings. During my last year, one of the students, Neville Webb, constructed a long gun by welding together numerous metal seven-pound jam jars, duly mounted on two motorbike wheels, so that "Wilkie" could receive a twenty-one gun salute, in the shape of deafening fireworks and a cascade of croquet balls.

I was also grateful to God for the enthusiasm and utter commitment and dedication of my tutor in the philosophy of religion, Ron Herniman, later Archdeacon of Barnstaple. His calling and gift was to teach us above all *to think*. He posed the deepest of questions, usually illustrated with gusto and enthusiasm. I recall lone tutorials with him, while he explained how the Empiricists viewed knowledge as coming through the senses. He would leap up from his chair, close the curtains, call attention to the darkness, and then dramatically open them again with a flourish, commenting, "So knowledge, Locke and Hume thought, comes through the senses, like light pouring through the window!"

I often sat two away from Ron at breakfast. There I could engage in his always informative discussions of philosophy or theology, but was also able to disengage if it was a familiar topic. He, too, was a providential gift for life: here was a living example of how to teach with total passion, and many clear, homely, illustrations.

Yet I learned at least as much from my two closest friends, Gavin Reid (later bishop of Maidstone) and Clive Porthouse (for many years vicar of his parish). We met after lunch every day, supposedly for social reasons, but in fact to put theology and the Church of England to rights. We debated every possible question, from the probable dates of Origen to clergy stipends and bishops. We were very firmly "Anglican, Reformed, and Evangelical" (in the proper sense), but were amused by, and incredulous at, some over-zealous brethren who would say, "When we Evangelicals take over the Church of England . . . ." They were just possibly nearer to the truth than we were, from the vantage-point of the 1990s.

We also had a ruthless, but necessary, elocution specialist. There was none of today's endless use of the glottal stop in place of the letter "t." Some might imagine that those from a less privileged background had the worst of it. But this was not the case. My good friend Ian Gardner was a polished Oxford graduate. But he had the college in stitches of laughter when Mr. Ripper requested him to stand in the gallery, and asked, in his actor's accent, "Are you aware that you always say, 'Nior,' instead of 'Nō'?" The answer was predictable. It was "Nior."

My good friend Gavin Reid had been commissioned in the Royal Air Force, and one of his favourite duties was to deliver lectures on the history of the Second World War. His special gift seemed to be to reproduce speeches of Adolf Hitler, with appropriate pseudo-Germanic accent, hysterical decibels, and convincing physical mannerisms. Most of the students had to join a gardening team, and Gavin Reid used to drill them ready for gardening action with appropriate Hitler-like speeches. Everyone did strenuous exercise in the college gardens, although my friend Godfrey Taylor achieved this by always sitting on the motor mower, while I achieved it by being college librarian.

Gavin Reid and I were also "co-conspirators" in the one of the groups that took part in the Christmas concert. One year we put on two sketches. Our major performance was one on *Treasure Island*. The principal was such a staunch right-wing Conservative that he had helped to drive trains during the 1926 General Strike. He was immensely patriotic. I was to play the part of Captain Smollett, who supposedly vaguely reflected the principal. I had to appear on stage wearing an eighteenth-century naval hat and uniform, proclaiming, "I am Captain Small-Nit, Church of England and Top Nation!" Gavin Reid appeared as Long John Silver, with strong Newton-type Devonshire dialect, and with a parrot and a wooden leg firmly attached to him. Eddie Gibbs, subsequently champion of Church Growth and a professor at Fuller Theological Seminary, was Jim the Cabin Boy.

Perhaps life could often be so very entertaining because devotion and prayer were stricter than that of many colleges or even other regimes today. In this respect this psychology reminded me of a medical school. The chapel bell summoned us every day at 7:10 a.m. Morning Prayer (in those days *always* Prayer Book) ended at around 7:45, to allow a time for silent prayer and meditation for three-quarters of an hour, until breakfast at 8:30. Lectures then began at 9 o'clock, and ceased at 12:55. We met in chapel again for ten minutes mid-day prayer. Lunch began at 1:15. Evening Prayer was said before the evening meal. Lights-out took place at 10:15 p.m.

Each of us was also allotted one or more training vicars. Providentially, again, my first was D. K. Dean, rector of Tooting, in South-West London. He had a parish of 20,000 people, yet maintained a card-index of virtually every family in the parish. He passionately believed in the C.P.A.S. motto, "The Gospel to Every Man's Door." Often teams consisting of the rector, his curates, and half-a-dozen lay people, would visit houses in the parish in the same road or street together. We were to talk not simply about "the church," but about Christ and the gospel. We then reported back, while D. K. Dean updated his records. In those days, wives were often at home in the afternoon.

Today many might doubt the rector's evangelistic methods. At Morning and Evening Prayer three psalms were sung, and the Prayer Book, including its rubrics about the Athanasian Creed, always rigidly observed. The church was packed. But I well remember South London accents dutifully reciting the three psalms, and wondering what sense they made of: "Whoy 'op ye so, ye 'igh 'ioos? This is God's 'ioo" (Ps 68:16, *Book of Common Prayer*, Coverdale translation); or, "Moab is my washpot; over Edom wioo I cast out my shoe" (Ps 60:8). I recall asking the rector where one could find these extra prayers for use as intercessions. He sternly replied, "My boy, everything you need is in the Prayer Book!"

To complement this, my second term with a training vicar was with John Potter, whose parish was near Archway in North London.

The vacations were varied, depending on what job was offered for that period. My best experience was at Shell Petroleum Efficiency Research. My office was labelled, "Enquiries," for which I had a list of names and room numbers. When anyone asked about a name, I had only to read out the room number on the list! One of my fellow ordinands was not so lucky: he was manning the lift, while revising New Testament Greek. A director exclaimed, "And what smutty little book is that?" My friend showed him his Greek New Testament!

During the last few months before ordination my Aunt Ethel became increasingly unwell. Eventually, after problems of double vision and other such problems, she was diagnosed as suffering from an advanced stage of cancer. She was duly taken into the Royal Marsden Hospital. I was greatly privileged to be present at her death. She drew enormous comfort from the old nineteenth-century hymn to the effect that in heaven, when it came to forgiveness of sins, even angels would have to "close their wings," while the redeemed alone could sing praise and thanks for forgiveness and redemption from the heart. Before she died, she bought me a black scarf for my ministry, which I have had all my life. Today it is adorned with the impressive crests or shields given to canons theologian of Leicester, and canons theologian of Southwell and Nottingham.

When the week prior to ordination arrived, two surprises awaited us. One was that Her Royal Highness Princess Margaret would be guest of the bishop and Cathedral on that occasion; the other was that the whole service would be televised. By this time Bishop Mervyn Stockwood had succeeded Bishop Bertram Simpson. I had been scheduled to read the Epistle, traditionally read by the youngest ordinand. But the bishop greeted me with surprising news. We were instructed to write three very long essays to be submitted to the bishop's chaplain, and I found that I had been judged first among the essayists of some thirty ordinands. Apparently, therefore, it would be my pleasant duty to read not the Epistle but the Gospel. So we practised duly with technicians, to establish sound level, and so forth.

On the great day we had to line up in procession long before the service was due to start. A desperate message was passed along the line of the procession of thirty to reach the officiating clergy. An ordinand had fallen victim to a most urgent call of nature. Would there be time to address this? The query was conveyed to the bishop. The answer was then passed back via the thirty ordinands in whispers, "Yes, but don't use the flush." The implication was that either the TV or H.R.H. Princess Margaret might pick up the sound, which would be unthinkable!

The service was duly solemn and memorable. Princess Margaret kindly presented the Bibles, in place of the bishop. Bishop Mervyn Stockwood loved theatre. One or two cynics asked, "When the psalmist says, 'The King of glory shall come in,' is he prophesying the advent of Bishop Mervyn Stockwood?'" In practice the bishop was very committed and diligent in caring for the welfare of his ordinands and in regularly praying for them. Later, after my ordination to the priesthood, Gavin Reid made the typical comment: "Well, now you can celebrate!"

Chapter 2

1960–63

A South-East London Curacy

WHEN I CAME TO look at the "curacy file" in my theological college, I was at first impressed to see the name of a very prominent and well-known vicar and sought-after speaker among those who were seeking a curate. I thought that it would be a great privilege to learn from him. In due course I arranged to see him and the parish. Nevertheless, when I consulted with friends, most warned me against becoming the curate of a famous vicar. I was urged that I would do better to work with someone less well known, but who would spend plenty of time with me. Since the interview with the famous figure had seemed indecisive, with great trepidation I phoned him up to decline the curacy, and to explain that I had accepted another. My hesitations were confirmed when he said to me, "Oh, I'm very surprised that you should choose to serve with *him*, when you might have had the chance of serving with *me!*"

I had meanwhile travelled to see the Reverend Leslie Shone, vicar of Holy Trinity, Sydenham, South-East London. He was modest and unassuming, and cared for a medium-sized parish of people from mixed backgrounds. We seemed to get on very well. I would be expected to engage in a full range of activities. He also promised to give me Mondays off to pursue studies for the M.Th. at King's College, London. I recall that the Southwark stipend was then £400 per year, although friends who went to the Guildford Diocese earned £550 a year for the same job. One bonus, however, was having a house, in effect, in the grounds of the church school, where I would teach twice each week, although the noise at playtimes was deafening.

I still have in my possession a scrapbook compiled by members of the Young Christians' Fellowship, and coordinated, I suspect, by the then Miss Gillian Hooper (now Mrs. Gillian Newman). It first records an event a week after ordination, namely a welcome Harvest Supper. Everything was delightful, but I thoughtlessly dropped a brick on this occasion. I have never especially liked a certain type of popular community singing. When I was asked to choose a song, I remember muttering, "Something as short as possible," and then wanting the ground to swallow me up.

Apart from regular sermons and conducting services, one of my main duties was to lead the Young Christians' Fellowship. I have a record of the programme from the scrapbook. Meetings were held either in the Church Hall lounge or in my house. We had to maintain a good variety of events to maintain interest. The December planning was immensely helped by the expectation of carol singing round the parish on several occasions.

Many of the older Youth Fellowship members were also Sunday school teachers. This was another major duty: I found myself being appointed as Sunday school superintendent. This meant many hours preparing elaborate visual aids, often from coloured paper, whereas today people simply use computer-generated images. In those days we also used flannel-graphs (i.e., paper or cardboard figures backed by something adhesive, and then moved around on any flannel background to illustrate a story). In those days, this was the height of our technology. Depending on what story had been chosen, the same figure could be used as Peter, Paul, Barnabas, or anyone else; the children did not seem to notice.

Holy Trinity Youth Fellowship

Once a month we held a family service, with an obligatory visual aid. I tried not to feel like a celebrity host, but it was obvious that the chosen and crafted visual aid was greeted and ranked with more overt enthusiasm and attention than the message that it illustrated. Today I blush at the crudity of some of my memories. For example, fountain pens were common at that time. I made a large-scale one that, in order to illustrate the Christian life in relation to Christ and the Holy Spirit, showed we could, like the pen, be Bought, Filled, and Used. Another was in effect a conjuring trick, in which ribbons representing human sin were, as if magically, made to disappear to illustrate the forgiveness of sins. For years I retained some visual aids, but eventually had to discard them, as they soon become dated, and some were theologically too crude.

At a relatively early stage in my curacy, I went to teach in the church school one morning, and felt an oncoming of pain. By mid-morning this had increased, and to my surprise and dismay, I was told by the medics that I needed to have an appendicectomy at once. An ambulance was called, which rushed me to King's College Hospital. The pain was reasonably moderate, so I was amazed at the sense of urgency in the hospital.

As soon as I arrived in hospital, I remembered that I already had an appointment to conduct a funeral that morning. I asked the nurses if I could urgently phone the undertaker. "Oh, your condition is not that bad," they said, misunderstanding my point; "there is no real risk to your life!" As I was rushed along the corridor on a trolley, all that I had with me was Albert Schweitzer's book, *The Mysticism of Paul the Apostle*. The medics seemed to be puzzled that I was reading Schweitzer on the way to the operating theatre; but reading-time constitutes a precious commodity for anyone in parish ministry who aims at the same time to gain a higher degree.

In the event, all went well, and I must again attribute my preservation to God's gracious providence. Two members of the Y.C.F., who were three-quarters through their medical training, Alan Disher and Duncan Colin-Jones, visited me in hospital, eating all my grapes, and causing vicious pain with riotous stories, repartee, and laughter.

In the parish, I received both the best and the worst of responses to sermons. Some helpful responses were very moving and positive. I recall discussing, "You are not far from the kingdom of God" with a very receptive parishioner. Other responses were less encouraging. One of the more offputting, though entirely well-intentioned, was "I found that interesting." My aim had not simply been to provide *interest*. Even today, after more than fifty years, I am still amazed at the kindly comment, "I really *learnt* something today," as if most preaching ministry had little to do with teaching.

The worst comment I ever received came when I accepted an invitation to preach in another parish on behalf of the Church Pastoral Aid Society. I had meant to explain the word *pastoral*, by trying to illustrate this from the Parable of the Good Shepherd and the Lost Sheep. I must have been an enormously bad communicator. For one lady commented at the door, "Thank you so much. I have been waiting for years to hear a sermon about the need to be kind to animals; at last you have given it!"

The church school was always a pleasure and delight. It provided ample opportunities for pastoral and human contact with families, mothers, and their children. It was also a fund of true stories about young children. I was told, for example, about the small child who would go nowhere near a church, but started kicking and screaming as soon as he was taken to a church door. Eventually someone persuaded him to look inside the church. In great bewilderment, he asked, "But where are all the babies? And where are all the cots?" A puzzled adult asked him, "Why should there be children there?" He replied, "I was taught that when you were baptized you were given to God. But I don't want to leave home; I want to stay with my Daddy and Mummy!"

The primary-age Sunday school playing
"What's the Time, Mr. Wolf?" with the Curate

One milestone with the Y.C.F. was to spend a week together on the Norfolk Broads. I was put in charge of the cruiser, as requiring less expertise than one of the five sailing boats. Alan Disher concocted some scurrilous mythology, such as making the curate responsible for a bent gear lever, or for crashing the cruiser as we entered Potter Higham Bridge, and, more credibly, for telling the crew that we were warned about "submerged plings," which on nearer approach turned out to be "Submerged Pilings."

I took my turn with the primary Sunday school. I can't remember exactly what we were doing, but I have a photograph in which I held hands with the children (perhaps difficult today with child protection!) under the caption, "What's the time, Mister Wolf?" We had various hikes in the Y.C.F., and two more sustained times away. One was at Mabledon, a country house in Kent, and another at The Hallams, Shamley Green, near Guildford. There, among other things, we saw over the new Guildford Cathedral. We also attended a Y.C.F. Rally in Euston, Central London.

I also recall outings with the Explorers. On one occasion we visited Chessington Zoo. We hired a double-decker bus, and I noted that the charge for children in those days (1960–63) was eight shillings and nine pence in old, pre-decimalized, money. We took several parents with us. It was less fraught than an earlier Sunday-School trip from Woking, when we left one child behind on the Isle of Wight, and a Sunday school teacher had to return to collect him again, while we all waited!

During my three years I conducted a number of weddings. Those which gave special pleasure were those which involved former Y.C.F. members, some of which were conducted by the vicar. One such was the marriage between Miss Carol Ditchburn, P.C.C. member and Pathfinder leader, and Dr. Duncan Colin-Jones, former president of the Barts Hospital Christian Union.

Funerals and cremations were altogether a different matter. We had the terrible system of a deanery rota. I was "on" every six or seven weeks, and around seven funerals or cremations lasted throughout the day. I would arrive at Hither Green Cemetery or Crematorium, with no prior knowledge of the deceased, and no prior visit to the family. The funeral director would simply murmur "brother" or "sister," and their gender was all that we knew of the deceased. One day the service might be for an eminent surgeon, with a chapel packed full of distinguished colleagues; another day it was effectively a pauper's funeral, with no one in attendance except perhaps only the funeral director. I always followed the Book of Common Prayer, although with Bible readings perhaps from J. B. Phillips. As the reading seemed to require, I always said something about the resurrection of the dead. In the case of a packed chapel I could often surmise who were overt or committed Christians. Many of the congregation gave me a stony stare as I stood at the door; but a few gripped my hand, and said, "Thank you for that," in a way that conveyed genuine approval and warmth.

I don't know any parish or deanery that follows this procedure today. Pre-funeral visits are mandatory, and those concerned usually come from within the parish. The one regrettable feature today seems to be the growing habit of asking for the music, "I did it My Way." People seem to imagine that this is a great compliment to the deceased; but it could surely be taken to mean, "He was a stubborn, self-sufficient, so and so, who thought he was always right about everything, and would never change his mind, even in the face of reason and argument."

The third set of occasional offices was that of baptism. I experienced nothing as unintentionally hilarious as one recounted by my friend Clive Porthouse. In those days, of course, we used only the Book of Common Prayer (1662). He carefully tried to train an East-End family in the vows and responses. When the public baptism arrived, he addressed the question to them posed by the exact words of the Prayer Book: "Dost thou, in the name of this Child, renounce the devil and all his works, the vain pomp and glory of the world, with all covetous desires of the same, and the carnal desires of the flesh, so that thou wilt not follow them?" A very lengthy pause followed this, as godparents nudged each other to respond. A loud East-end bass voice at last boomed out in answer: "I recommend them all!"

By comparison, my services were fairly uneventful. In the case of babies, I rigidly followed our former college principal's mantra: "Baby's head to left elbow; baby's bottom to left hand!" Then, in multiple baptism services, one only had to match the appropriate baby to the appropriate name, however unusual or bizarre. By that time I had read the philosopher J. L. Austin's speculative hypothesis about speech acts. Austin asked, would it constitute an effective speech act if the clergyman uttered, "I baptize this infant 2704"? (*How to Do Things with Words*. Clarendon, 1962, 35.)

I have so far not mentioned my engagement to be married to Rosemary. She was from the Royal Academy of Music, and the Y.C.F. For a single male curate to try to court a young lady is always a tricky business.

We managed to keep our meetings unknown, and travelled from time to time quietly, often separately, to Hayes Common in Kent. I recall the day when Rosemary appeared at the Y.C.F. wearing her engagement ring. The Y.C.F. was supportive and enthusiastic, but then they asked: "To whom are you engaged?" I remember the reaction when she replied, "To the curate!" There was a stunned silence, followed by, "to *him?!*" The other related memory is that of my last Sunday. Everyone had nice, flattering, things to say. Finally it was the turn of the vicar. Looking immensely solemn and serious, he said, "He does not deserve a farewell gift." There followed a long pause. He then added, "We've already given him Rosemary; he ought to be satisfied with that!"

Rosemary and I were able to spend one weekend together while we were engaged. We went to stay with Godfrey and Daphne Taylor (he of the motor mower fame) at Herne Bay. They had just bought a new puppy. It was, of course, not house-trained. When it could not avoid leaving unwelcome evidence of its lack of training, Godfrey would quote the book of Revelation, chapter 19: "the mark of the beast." He has often been appointed to seaside parishes from Herne Bay to Guernsey. "Don't laugh," said Gavin Reid, "He is keeping the Catholics out of England."

Our vicar, Leslie Shone, had two favourite pieces of humour. When crossing a road, he used often to murmur, "Hurry up! The Creed tells us that there are only the quick and the dead." When watching the treasurer count the collection, he would often quote the words in 2 Timothy 4:14 (AV/KJB): "Alexander the coppersmith hath done me great harm." I had never quite recovered from our first staff meeting, when he was briefing me about our Sunday-school teachers. I asked him who taught the very youngest. I was shattered when I thought he said, "Margaret and I," for I could not imagine him amidst the crowd of four- or five-year-olds. But I need not have been so incredulous. What he had actually said was: "Margaret Nye."

I had time to spend some days off (in theory, every Monday) with friends. I regularly saw Clive Porthouse, who was curate in Leyton, East London. His vicar was obsessed with the puritans and their writings in books published by the Banner of Truth. I recall hearing him addressing an East-End congregation with direct quotations from these seventeenth-century writings. He addressed his congregation, "If he hath a distemper, I trow, . . ." in full expectation of performing an intelligible communication. On the other hand, my friend, who had taken an honours BD, was allowed, he said, to excel only at woodwork. The curate's lot in those days was very different from today. I recall stoking the boiler, clearing away snow, and undertaking other similar tasks.

One day Clive and I nearly attended a Picasso exhibition in London. After we had parked hats and coats, Clive enquired about the price for admission. When the attendant stated, "Three shillings and six pence" (in 1961), my blunt Northern friend exclaimed: "Eh! Not worth it!," and to my embarrassment we had to return to collect our hats and coats. He was also beginning to court his wife-to-be, Marion. But at first, when he rang the bell by their front door, Marion simply escaped through the back door.

I took my turn in preaching in other churches. This sometimes led to situations which I had not experienced before. Ours was the only Evangelical church in a deanery of seventeen churches. When I visited one Anglo-Catholic church, I heard the choir pleading with the vicar to make the Communion Service into a "Solemn Mass." To my surprise, he explained to me that in practice this simply meant many more "smells and bells" than they usually had. I experienced, of course, being "censored" by a server who wore an over-elaborate attire, both in the prayers and on my way to the pulpit. In spite of this, I held my nerve in preaching on the final Advent on Advent Sunday. I was grateful that Calvin's emphasis on the parity of Word and Sacrament found expression in my wearing identical robes for Holy Communion and Morning and Evening Prayer!

So my time in Sydenham, South London, drew to a close. My next appointment was a delight, and was to take me, with Rosemary, to Bristol. The principal of the College, then called Tyndale Hall Theological College, phoned me one night at around 11 p.m. His cool but cheery voice simply said, "I gather that you are interested in lecturing in theology, especially in the context of the church. Would you like to come and see us?" I could barely contain my excitement. Thus began my transition to academia, and in the city of Bristol, effectively the capital city of the West of England. The last event at Holy Trinity, Sydenham, was to be my wedding to Rosemary, except when I re-visited the church for a special occasion many years later.

Our wedding, September 21st 1963

Our wedding, with my mother, Hilda, my uncle, Dr. Ernest Kevan, principal of London Bible College (now London School of Theology), and Rosemary's parents, Ernest and Elsie Harman

Chapter 3

1963–70

Academia and the Church in Bristol

FOR MY INTERVIEW I travelled by train from Paddington to Bristol Temple Meads, and took a bus from the station to Pembroke Road, Clifton. There, first of all, I met the Reverend Stafford Wright. I knew that he lectured in Old Testament and psychology. When he therefore gave me a long, assessing, penetrating, gaze, I was determined not to be the first to shift eye-contact. Thereafter the interview was extremely pleasant, and at times humorous. At the end he gave me the impression that he had almost already decided to appoint me. But he asked whether I would like to meet the rest of the teaching staff.

The vice-principal was the Reverend John Wenham, with whom I was later to become a close friend. He was the author of the famous book *The Elements of New Testament Greek,* which became a standard first-year textbook in many universities and theological colleges. Like Stafford Wright, he was a modest and frugal man, and I remember his using black Indian ink to attempt to restore part of the worn pattern of a carpet in his house. I think I met two other members of the teaching staff, who quizzed me about some of my theological views.

In the event, Stafford Wright duly appointed me. I discovered that it would in fact be a double job, involving both teaching at the theological college, and becoming what the University of Bristol called "A Recognized Teacher in Theology." This would be a special delight, since I was drawn both to the college, with its pastoral responsibilities, and to university life, with its greater opportunities for research and perhaps collaboration.

The beginning of the autumn term began only a few days after my wedding to Rosemary. Hence, we decided to take a very short honeymoon at what I had imagined would be a seaside town near Bristol. In the event, I booked us into a charming room in a hotel at Swanage, Dorset. It was adjacent to the sea, indeed virtually on the sea-edge. But I had not studied the railway network. Only when it was too late to re-book did I realize that there was apparently no direct or easy trainline between Swanage and Bristol.

Our hasty return to Bristol therefore involved a fairly lengthy taxi ride. We arrived at Tyndale Hall, breathless from our journey, to the first evening meal of the term. Stafford Wright greeted me with the words, "Oh, you are here already. Knowing the date of your wedding, I really had not expected you to arrive for some time!" From then on I came to understand that "Staffie," as we all called him, was immensely relaxed. I recall seeing somewhere a sheet labelled "College Rules," on which there was virtually only one, namely, "Students are required not to climb on the roofs of the College."

I discovered that I was either of equal age to many of the students, or possibly even younger than some. But in 1963 all the students addressed me as "Sir," and never used my Christian name, at least to my face. When I lectured on New Testament set books, I learnt that only theological graduates had ever been exposed to serious exegesis. On the other hand, many theological graduates had never really appreciated that a biblical exposition could carry with it many practical, pastoral, applications to life.

I relished conversations at breakfast with the students. Conversation could switch quickly between pastoral and parish subjects and theological issues of importance. Lunch was served at a high table with other members of the teaching staff. Again, conversation switched between theology and global politics. Both meals provided a wonderful way of becoming friends with both staff and students. Supper took place after evening chapel, when I was free to eat with Rosemary.

I had to travel from Bristol to London to undergo the oral exam for the M.Th., which was held only once a year, even though the 50,000-word thesis had been submitted beforehand. In the days before computers, my thesis had been typed with four carbon copies. Any mistakes would have to be rectified inconspicuously on four copies (three to be submitted, one to be at hand for reference), and Greek had to be written by hand (with accents) by black Indian ink. There was no room for error.

Professor Nineham chaired the oral examination, and I had the privilege of being examined by Professor Charlie Moule of Cambridge as the external examiner. I arrived at King's College so early that I had time to kill. I therefore took a few minutes in St. Clement Dane's Chapel, near the junction of Strand and Fleet Street. But by the time I returned, the examiners were waiting, and I was invited to begin the oral earlier than was formally scheduled. Thus, instead of arriving calm, cool, and collected, I arrived hot and flustered. I was relieved to receive good news in due course.

The university professor at Bristol, Kenneth Grayston, had recently been appointed as Bristol's first professor of theology. Hitherto the university's theology teachers had been the lecturers appointed to the five theological colleges. In some ways it was a delicate stage of transition. Some colleagues at other colleges had been used to the Oxford system, and complained to me that a professor should be *primus inter pares*, not "boss," as in many civic universities. My worst task emerged when the professor fell out with one of my part-time colleagues over the status of what were often regarded as the more marginal books on the edge of the New Testament canon. In the end, neither wished willingly to communicate with the other, and I was left to carry messages between them.

In spite of our being such a young department, in those days we were accorded some five or so external examiners for the Bristol BA in Theology. I recall each sub-discipline being represented around the table. Later, when I taught at Sheffield, the department was allowed only one external examiner. At Bristol, I do not remember being involved in examining any joint honours subject; we were usually simply informed of results.

Steadily the Department of Theology appointed more full-time lecturers, beginning with Dr. Kent. This was accompanied by a parallel marginalization of the theological colleges, and contributed to my eventual move from Bristol to Sheffield. I was, however, encouraged to supervise higher degrees, in addition to teaching for the Bristol BA on "The Hellenistic Church."

Meanwhile Tyndale Hall had a smaller full-time staff than could easily match the large variety of degrees and courses for which we taught. These included the Bristol BA, the London BD, the London Diploma in Theology, and the General Ordination Examination. At one stage a crisis emerged between the council and teaching staff at our sister college, Clifton Theological College, Stoke Bishop. Two of us found ourselves teaching a variety of subjects, which ranged from New Testament set texts to philosophy of religion, some for the ordination exam, and others for degree courses. We also taught in a third college, Dalton House, Bristol, which served the training of deaconesses. Eventually there were firm plans to merge these three colleges, and I can claim the honour of first proposing to Stafford Wright that the one merged college should be called Trinity College. This name was accepted by all parties, and remains the shared name today.

Tyndale Theological College; from 1963 to 1967 our flat was on the middle floor of the diagonal building on the corner of Pembroke Road.

I recall numerous "Christmas concerts," in which students would impersonate staff, and often come up with some gems of sketches. Some used material from Bristol, such as the well-known reference to Bristle phrases such as, "Yere 'tis," and, "Have you seen the famous warship 'Grape Written'?" Others used skits or take-offs on popular advertisements. One of the latter occurred when Chris Hill drank from what was known to have laxative effects. Using a brilliant Bernard Miles-cum-Bristol accent, he solemnly and slowly pronounced, "Looks good; tastes good; and (more rapidly) by golly it does you good"—as he frantically rushed off the stage in mock-consternation!

Staffie's study always caused amusement. I well remember standing in the hall and main entrance to the college, where his door was close at hand. Somehow he managed to lecture throughout the mornings, and to work in his house in the afternoons. He would therefore dictate letters on a very old-fashioned tape-recording machine, which his secretary evidently needed to play at full volume. His voice would come piercing through the door into the hallway, duly amplified. We might hear some such letter as this: "Strictly Confidential: Dear bishop, I recommend this student with some hesitations. Confidentially . . . ."

One fruitful source of instruction and amusement was our sermon classes. One resident teacher of the college would travel with six or seven students to churches broadly within the Bristol area. We would listen to the sermon given by a student, and then discuss the sermon after the service, either with or without the local vicar and one or two laypeople.

One of the churches that provided most amusement was St. John-on-the-Wall, in the city of Bristol. David Gregg recounts a fair picture: "It was the *narrowest* church imaginable [in both senses]. Literally set within the city wall, it has a long aisle while seating four-abreast on each side." This church was so conservative and traditional that the liturgy was conducted by a clergyman robed in a black Geneva gown. David Gregg continues, "Morning and Evening Prayer ended at 'The Grace,' and the minister then had to rush into the vestry (behind the Communion table), shed his cassock and surplice, and re-appear (like the pantomime demon out of his trapdoor) in the pulpit, set in the side-wall alongside the sanctuary." To my knowledge, it was one of only three "black-gown" churches in England in 1963. The service ended with the National Anthem. The elderly vicar always announced it with the oddly pronounced "s's": "God shave the Queen." Psalms were always said, not sung, to show reverence for Scripture, although the Gloria at the end of each psalm was duly sung. In the pulpit the sermon was timed not by a watch or clock, but by an *hour glass*!

There were two huge brass lecterns, one for the Old Testament, and the other for the New. One of the churchwardens, David Gregg recalls, would mount the steps, turn the brass lectern round "with a loud screeching noise, . . . and begin in a genuine Long John Silver accent . . . 'Tonight's readin' iz from fi'ty-third cha'ter, book of Oisoial—'oo 'ath b'lieved arr report, and t'hoom iz the arm o' the Lord revealed?'" At a sermon class, conducted by John Wenham, it was announced that the vicar had specifically asked for something in the preaching to be a challenge for unbelievers. John Wenham commented, "To imagine unbelievers at John-on-the-Wall defies the imagination beyond credulity!"

At the opposite extreme, we used to visit a parish church in Locking, Somerset, where one of our part-time teaching staff was also the vicar. He used to express his dismay if the students were too lengthy. On one particular occasion, he vented his annoyance with one student by commenting, "A forty-minute sermon is really bad enough; but forty minutes on the devil is intolerable!" At other times, as Frank Beech recalled, he was heard to observe, "The general public should be protected from people like you!"; "This sermon is like a bucket full of liquorice all sorts"; and "Brilliant in parts, but in other places I wish you had taken up knitting."

On the question of length, John Wenham was always helpful. His maxim was as follows: if sermon was good and short, that was best of all; if it was good and long, the congregation might just accept it; if it was short and bad, the congregation might reflect, "He is only a young man starting off." But if it was long and bad, the congregation will find no excuse. This reminded me of the village squire who first placed the gold sovereign in full view of the preacher. After ten minutes he exchanged it for a half sovereign; after a quarter of an hour for a crown; and after twenty minutes, for a half-a-crown (today, about twelve pence).

We visited a variety of churches. Some were extreme in the Anglo-Catholic tradition. Hence one Evangelical student asked the wife of the Anglo-Catholic vicar to coach him in that church's normal practices. David Gregg recalls, "When he asked her if he had followed the ritual adequately, she replied, 'Very good, really, but my husband doesn't usually *wear* the bookmarks!'"

The vicar of St. Philip and St Jacob, or "Pip 'n J," as it became known, was Malcolm Widdecombe, known later as the brother of Anne Widdecombe, M.P. He belonged firmly, even in 1963, to the "no robes for clergy" brigade. So unknown to me, he had told the congregation that I would be presiding at Communion, knowing full well that I would not have robes with me, and not offering to provide any! Against my conscience and will, I found myself presiding at Prayer Book Communion, wearing a dog collar, but also, for the first and last time, a plain suit! Malcolm was always known as an unconventional and colourful character at Tyndale Hall well before my arrival. Stafford Wright observed of him, "He will either be a total disaster or absolutely brilliant." In the event the second proved to be the case. Under his ministry "Pip n' J" prospered and gave massive sums to overseas missions and Christian Aid, took food and goodies to down and outs, and Malcolm became rural dean of Bristol, and honorary canon of Bristol Cathedral. David Gregg recalls that Malcolm was also an expert in publicity, even inveigling a local television crew to film their activities. When Malcolm and the TV crew stumbled on the dead body of a down-and-out, this made the main spot on the next day's news bulletins.

I used to undertake parish-type duties while lecturing. Here I have conducted the wedding of two friends, Jason and Jean Abdelnoor, at Redland Church, which we also attended when possible

Those who drove us to the churches were often entertaining. George Deacon was an older ordinand, who had a strong Bristol accent. When he encountered examples of bad drivers, he would sound his horn, observing, "Oi loik to giv'em a littoo smack, as if they were nawdy children, which they are, reely." At least we felt safe with George. One volunteer driver used to take us at high speed over the crest of hills through very narrow lanes, which were usually between villages in the Diocese of Bath and Wells.

Comments after the students conducted Evening Prayer were also sometimes memorable. Staffie had virtually one comment for almost everyone. The Prayer Book Collect for the Queen contains the petition, "Most heartily we beseech Thee with Thy favour to behold our most gracious Sovereign Lady, Queen Elizabeth." Whatever slips the student minister may have committed, Staffie would choose as his first or only comment, "Not, 'We beseech Thee, with Thy favour, to behold'; but 'with Thy favour to behold.'"

Since I was a member of the teaching staff (for some time as chaplain), we several times took students with us to lead missions. In 1965 we travelled to Christ Church, Surbiton (later to be made famous by Penelope Keith in *The Good Life*). Students came from Tyndale Hall and Dalton House, and we worked closely with the vicar, Mr. J. Carpenter, the curate, Eddie Shiras (later Archdeacon of Northolt), and eleven people from Christ Church. The bishop of Kingston, Rt. Revd. W. P. Gilpin, opened the week by preaching on the first Sunday, and I preached on the closing Sunday evening. Our visiting and speaking was well received. After all, we were in polite, suburban, Surbiton.

I am tempted to relate a story that nowadays would be called "politically incorrect." On our way back from a city church, one Sunday, we were all on foot. Mini-skirts had recently come into fashion. That day they seemed to have been raised to new heights (in both senses). Recalling no doubt a recent Greek lesson, David James exclaimed, "You can't call that a mini-skirt; it's more like a micro-skirt." In those days even the ladies who were training at Dalton House wore mini-skirts.

On the more personal side, 1964, 1966, and 1969, witnessed the birth of our three children, Stephen, Linda, and Martin. Since Stephen was Rosemary's first, he was delivered in St. Brenda's Nursing Home, Clifton. I had been told to wait for news at home. To my joy, St. Brenda's phoned me to say that all was well, and I shall always be grateful for the words of the college matron, Lillian Austin, as I rushed off on my bicycle: "Don't kill yourself! Rosemary would not appreciate that!" Our second and third children were born at home, while I was present at their births. We lived in a flat in the College when Linda was born, and I wondered whether some of the students could hear the progress of events. College premises made overheard conversations too easy. Before my arrival the publicly dignified Dr. Jim Packer lived in a college flat. He was married to Kit. The students loved to recount hearing Kit cry, "Put me down, Jim!" Visual sighting was as bad. I recall embracing Rosemary, to the accompaniment of thunderous student cheers from the window that (I had not realized) overlooked us!

On the academic side, all the teaching staff participated in the Bristol Theological Society. This provided an excellent opportunity to debate really serious issues in theology, and to promote friendship with colleagues in other colleges. On one occasion the principal of the Congregational College, announced, "There is no truth in the rumour that this college is going to close." Almost inevitably a few months or so later their closure was announced.

Colin Brown, a close colleague, used to travel with me to conferences. He would later become a professor at Fuller Theological Seminary in Pasadena, California. We went, for example, to Oxford for Professor Sparks' conference on the Four Gospels. But the real highlight came when I attended alone the Society for the Study of Theology in 1969, I think at Birmingham. The two professorial brothers, Richard Hanson of Manchester and Anthony Hanson of Hull, were there. Always colourful, and known for blunt and pungent comments, they had just listened with dismay to a British professor's disappointing paper. This was meant, no doubt, to be an exploration in the phenomenology of religion. It ended up simply as: "Muslims do this; Hindus do that." The Hanson brothers were heard to say, in effect, to Wolfhart Pannenberg, "We hope that you will not take that paper as representative of what we British professors would normally do!"

Pannenberg informed me that he and his wife planned to visit Bristol, and asked whether I knew of any hotel there that I could recommend? I offered either to suggest a hotel, or to accommodate them in our home, and to my surprise they accepted our hospitality. It proved to be a marvellous occasion. We had some stimulating theological conversations, and I even had the temerity to ask if they would like to join us for our regular family prayers, which they did.

Halfway through the stay, Professor Pannenberg asked, "Vere do you usually take your vife for dinner? Ve voult like to take you for a meal." I had never taken Rosemary to anywhere that would be fit for the Pannenbergs. So while they were away for the day, I scouted round restaurants in Bristol and took some advice. We found a good-quality but not exorbitant inn, and enjoyed an utterly relaxed and pleasant evening. This visit indelibly marked my thinking, for Pannenberg remains one of the two theologians who has most influenced me, the other being Jürgen Moltmann. Some years later I was able to enjoy much more of his company, when he kindly visited Nottingham.

I often used to work closely with Colin Brown while we were both at Bristol. I remember once his commenting on the many courses that we taught. I recall his saying, quite rightly, "At times it seems as if you and I are lecturing on virtually everything, with the exception of the Old Testament and psychology, which Staffie teaches." In fact, we were both passionately interested in every branch of theology, he especially in history, and I especially in theological language. We were both interested in philosophy, modern theology, and biblical studies, and our multiple courses gave us every opportunity to explore them. Many years later, when I travelled to Fuller as visiting professor, students told me that two Englishmen, Colin Brown and Leslie Allen, represented the very best of Fuller's teachers!

In those days, George's Bookshop at the top of Park Street was an excellent resource for theological books. I was amazed when some twenty-five years later I was scouring the country for a rare book, and phoned up George's. The delightful Bristolian voice asked on the telephone whether I was the same Thiselton as he used to serve regularly during the 1960s. In fact, all theological books in Bristol, as far as I knew, were bought either at George's or SPCK, both in Park Street. In those days we always used to scramble for the annual book sale at SPCK.

As the years went by, there was often useful theological collaboration between the teaching staff of the five theological colleges and with the university full-time staff. But this never approached the degree of close collaboration that I would enjoy at Sheffield, nor did it ever recapture an earlier era at Bristol when Alec Motyer, Michael Farrer, Peter Dawes, and Jim Innes, taught at Clifton.

This, however, was only one reason why, when Sheffield University offered to appoint me, I grabbed the opportunity with both hands. The dominant problem at Bristol was the huge mass of teaching a wide variety of courses, many part of the diverse syllabi of different universities. Clearly this meant a corresponding reduction of time for research and writing. In addition, there were endless rounds of staff meetings, working-parties, preaching, sermon-classes, tutorials, meetings in London, as well as College meetings. By contrast, when I was appointed to Sheffield, Professor James Atkinson managed the department with only one staff meeting per term! We also taught to one single degree syllabus. The only parity was supervising higher degrees in the two universities.

1963–70

Professor James Atkinson, DTheol, DD,
professor of biblical studies at Sheffield University,
friend, mentor, and role-model

Virtually all my reading and research at Bristol had been geared to speaking engagements and academic papers. I managed to write three small articles on Kierkegaard, Tillich, and Hermeneutics, which were all published in *The Churchman*. The one really significant piece of research began as a paper at Oxford on Ernst Fuchs, and ended up as an article for the *Scottish Journal of Theology* under the title: "The Parables as Language Event: Some Comments on Fuchs' Hermeneutics in the Light of Linguistic Philosophy" (vol. 23, 1970, pp. 437–68). It was later re-printed in *Thiselton on Hermeneutics* (Eerdmans and Ashgate, 2006, pp. 414–40), with forty-one other articles.

It was not surprising that, in spite of future difficulties about housing and the loss of some close friends, I had no hesitation about moving to Sheffield University. There, away from the hectic round and frenetic pace of English theological colleges, I was to form a special bond with Professor James Atkinson, and with other colleagues.

Chapter 4

1970–85
University and Church in Sheffield (and London)

FORTUNATELY FOR ME, IT emerged that Professor Atkinson, who chaired the Appointing Committee, shared my enthusiasm for 1 Corinthians. During the interview of question and answer, much of the material seemed to turn on 1 Corinthians, and we at once seemed to strike up a rapport. I had tried to prepare for the interview by revising my material, among other things, on Fuchs, Hermeneutical Theory, and Wittgenstein, but most of the committee seemed not to have any interest in them! Although I learnt much later that there were some discordant voices on the committee, in the event, I was duly appointed. In the first instance this appointment was to the Sir Henry Stephenson Research Fellowship, which allowed up to six hours teaching in the university each week, and was held initially for two years, on a renewal basis.

Since we had lived in the college house up until then, I had the new (for me) task of exploring renting a house. Purchase would not have been realistic for perhaps as short a period as two years. I had heard that some excellent council houses were empty, and innocently phoned the Council Housing Department. I don't know which of us felt the greater shock and outrage: the Housing Department, to be phoned by someone who was not even on the housing waiting-list, and had never even corresponded with the council; or me, who learned that they would rather have some of their best houses empty, than over-ride a convoluted bureaucratic housing procedure of waiting lists. The Labour council had flung me into the arms of a private landlord!

I then phoned a number of Sheffield clergy to ask whether they could help with my seeking to rent a house; but I drew a blank, and met with some no-replies. The Reverend Harold Everest, however, vicar of St. John's Park, East Sheffield, was about to lose two curates, Rev. John Sweed and Rev. Ian Neil. John Sweed, to our great relief, replied at once to say that although the vicar was on holiday, and could not be reached, he would ask him about it on his return. When he left Sheffield, John Sweed would be leaving a vacant house at 261 Granville Road. This was providential in two ways: for us, it would provide us with a house; and for the vicar, it offered immediate clerical staffing to the parish, while the curacy vacancies dragged on.

It was decided that we could occupy 261 Granville Road for a short time, in exchange for taking on the Sunday duties of the other departing curate, Jim Neil, who had been chaplain to the Park Hill flats. These were a multi-storey block of council flats in East-central Sheffield. This would involve the kind of ministry of which I had little or no prior experience. In the end, this provided both a house and new pastoral experience for some fourteen months. It was another gift of providence.

For me, the year was full of interesting surprises. My first pastoral problem involved adjudicating the charge that a member of the congregation had stolen coins from the collection plate! Second, I was then faced with appointing a "May Queen," for which there was fierce inter-family competition. Third, I had inherited from Jim Neil such so-called hymns as "Gimme oonction in my goompion, so Ah foonction," sung to the tune of: "Give me joy in my heart, keep me praising"! So-called Fresh Expressions or Messy Church would not appear on the horizon until thirty years later.

From a congregation of theological students who wanted theologically profound sermons, I needed to follow the style indicated by Harold Everest. He chose simple and direct approaches for his ten-minute sermons. One, which I recall, involved "Herod, the King of Spades; Pilate, the King of Diamonds; the centurion, the King of Clubs; and Jesus, the King of Hearts." As Professor F. F. Bruce once wrote concerning my first book on hermeneutics, "It was an education."

I found the university students at Sheffield, who came from a variety of backgrounds, eager to learn in my tutorials, in which we especially discussed First Corinthians. The one exception was an exchange student from the United States of America, who did her very utmost to introduce discussions on feminism at every possible turn on the basis of every possible verse. Politicians might call this a one-issue agenda. The second and third year students were a delight. With Professor Atkinson's active encouragement, several were considering ordination, church work, or teaching religious studies, which at once provided a special bond with them.

The Senior Common Room Club was immensely inviting and civilized, and provided good interaction with various teaching staff, especially those in philosophy and linguistics. Very soon I was not only attending the Sheffield Philosophical Society, but also even gave a paper on Wittgenstein at one of its meetings. In early December I was even conducting regular interviews for joint-honours admissions in biblical studies and philosophy. I recall conducting a joint-honours interview with Professor Peter Nidditch, the Locke specialist, in which the candidate appeared incredibly lifeless and bored. Eventually we asked him whether he really wanted to take a degree at Sheffield or not. He replied, "Not really, I would much rather go into the army." When we asked, "Then why are you here?" he replied, "Because my parents would be furious if I wasn't." When we asked, "Would you like us to say 'Reject,' then?" he suddenly came to life, and said "Yes please; that would be terrific!"

Several months later I had a delightful surprise. The Faculty of Arts allocated to our Department of Biblical Studies an additional permanent lecturer's post in New Testament. I had no hesitation in applying for the post. Four candidates were selected for a short-list from a longer one. All were well qualified, and when I learned about the competition, I knew that anything could happen. This time the dean of Arts chaired the Appointing Committee. I was fortunate in having taken on interviewing for admissions, and being known in the department and faculty. At all events, to my unbounded joy I was appointed. David Clines said on my appointment: "Welcome to the crummiest department in the country." We all knew that this was ironic, because it was in fact a fine, go-ahead, friendly, department. The next time I was to hear the word "crummy" of a faculty would be in the 1990s, when Professor John Webster welcomed us to his "crummy" Faculty of Theology at Oxford!

Under the leadership of James Atkinson, the ethos was warm, intimate, supportive, and friendly. This extended to teaching staff and students. Those who were on joint-honours degrees in which the other department was very large, for example Biblical Studies and English, either looked with envy on our personal knowledge of each student, or decided to transfer to Biblical Studies Single Honours at the end of their first year.

My reading and research took off with excellent, warm, and friendly colleagues in Philosophy and in Linguistics. This helped me to write a number of articles. Although Professor Nidditch was both Jewish and nominally agnostic, he greatly respected our department, and introduced me to John Locke's book, *Notes of the Epistles of Paul*. Nigel Gotteri in Linguistics was Eastern Orthodox, and all staff there were most hospitable. It was not long before I was lecturing in the Department of Linguistics on semantics. I also gave joint-supervisions to PhD students with Peter Nidditch or Meirlys Lewis in Philosophy on Wittgenstein, and with Nigel Gotteri on linguistics, semantics, and speech acts.

In the providence of God, once again, our rented house had been available for as long as fourteen months. The permanent appointment meant that we could now buy a house. James Atkinson added his advice to our decision to purchase a house in Roslin Road, near to the university, and virtually on the 52 bus route from the university.

Thus began our regular custom of inviting a number of students to Sunday afternoon tea. This provided some ready long-term friendships. The one problem arose when Rosemary asked about expected numbers. Often I would reply, "ten" or "eleven." But Rosemary then asked, "How many are men?" This mattered because men required massive quantities of food, while the women students ate very little indeed. I had learned from D. K. Dean that one could easily impose a *terminus ad quem* by stating boldly: "By the way, we leave for church at six o'clock; you are welcome to come, if you want!" Over the years I learned how much entry to our home had meant to students who were away from theirs.

Friendships were also formed by both staff and students sharing in Christmas end-of-term reviews. I mounted an item which stemmed from my lectures. At the beginning I lectured for six or seven hours each week. I took first-year Greek, and lectured to second and third-year students in New Testament literature: the Synoptic Gospels; Pauline theology; the Epistle to the Hebrews; and New Testament history. This last provided a spoof illustration of the course. I borrowed an old epidiascope, which could project cut-outs or pictures onto a screen. I cut out, for example, a picture of a builder or modern labourer in a cloth cap (obligatory in Yorkshire), with a wheel-barrow loaded with bricks, and displayed the historically accurate caption: "Herod was a great builder!" Herod and his illicit women-friends could come from modern Nice or Monte Carlo. My old Sunday-school flannelgraphs, or alternatively modern soldiery, could readily simulate Roman legions.

As time passed I took my turn at interviewing for joint-honours admissions in biblical studies and ancient history, Latin, or Greek. Ancient history was the most fun. The professor of ancient history, Derek Mozley, interviewed the candidates first, and gave them each a brown envelope summarizing his initial verdict before discussion. Occasionally we had candidates who seemed the opposite of lively. Sometimes on such occasions, the envelope contained only two words: "Wet Lettuce."

Over the years the high-speed lifts in the Arts Tower became increasingly crowded, as the university turned lecture rooms on the upper floors to staff offices, and located lectures in the basement. We were on the tenth floor. In vain we called for the lift, simply to find it full, after an inordinate wait. The only other way of climbing to the nineteenth floor or descending to the basement (apart from stairs) was to use the "paternoster lift." This moved slowly enough to allow those fully fit to jump on and off at the desired floor. The problem was the safety trip-wire mechanism, which brought the entire rotating lift for nineteen floors to a sudden, abrupt, stop, in the event of an accident. The trouble was that for the first five weeks of term, new students repeatedly tripped the safety wire, leaving everyone stranded on some half-way house of varying degrees. The compensation was to observe members of staff (or students) either jumping from heights barely within their capacity, and nursing bruised feet, or trying painstakingly to crawl upwards to a floor which was barely, if at all, within reach.

By standing for election to the Non-Professorial Staff Association, I managed to become elected to the Senate as well as to the Board of the Faculty of Arts for some considerable time. Both were useful and also entertaining. Competition for faculty elections was fierce. Yet when the Wednesday afternoon of a Faculty Board arrived, one could hear howls of frustration: "Oh heck (or more accurately, oh ****), not *another* Faculty Board!"

At the Senate we did not wear gowns, as we did at Durham. But types of attire made sectional uniforms. Medical professors, classicists, and theologians, wore smart dark suits. Those from Sociology wore jeans and tea-shirts. Those from Chemistry found an intermediate compromise. I always enjoyed listening to our professor of ancient history, whose specialism was rhetoric, first carefully putting the opposite case from what he wanted, so that he could then demolish it. The snag was that some members of Senate would switch off or drift off before the second part of the rhetoric had been completed.

I would then enter an entirely different world when I had to travel to London for the Church of England's Faith and Order Advisory Group (FOAG), the Council for National Academic Awards (CNAA), and the Church of England Evangelical Council (CEEC). The bishop of Chichester, Eric Kemp, chaired FOAG; John Stott chaired the CEEC; David Jenkins and then Kenneth Wilson chaired the Board of Theological Studies for CNAA. All three bodies had some colourful members. FOAG contained some strong and robust personalities. Miss Christian Howard of Castle Howard in Yorkshire was one such. She was always very concerned about how much of our work could "get through Synod." For a short period Canon Cheslin Jones of Pusey House, recently of the Doctrine Commission, was another lively and colourful member. I recall his addressing Miss Howard through the chair with heavy sarcasm: "I do apologize, chairman. I had not thought much about the General Synod. I am afraid I thought that we were here simply to *reach the truth*." One of the two, as the chairman predicted, would resign before the next meeting; it was Canon Jones.

Probably the most colourful person on Church of England Evangelical Council (CEEC) was Professor (ex-Colonel) Norman Anderson. His interventions operated exactly like his peeling and cutting of a lunchtime apple: brief, efficient, crisp, and deadly. I don't remember anyone disagreeing with him. It was a much more progressive body than it has become in recent years. I think that this was because John Stott and Norman Anderson were so highly respected that a little speculation and flexibility was deemed acceptable.

The fun with CNAA was largely travelling to inspect polytechnics, colleges of higher education, and theological colleges to check whether they matched CNAA criteria. Members and inspection teams were not paid any salary, but were paid first class fares and excellent hotel accommodation. My one disappointment was that we would usually meet so late in the evenings, and then hold a briefing session, that by the time we were ready to begin dinner at our four-star hotel, it would probably be around 9 o'clock, and I was almost too tired to eat. Then we had a very early morning, usually collected from the hotel by the minibus of the college or polytechnic, and welcomed by an anxious principal and staff. On the whole the worst of the colleges were those that had "Quality Assurance Departments."

On one memorable occasion we inspected an Anglican theological college with David Jenkins in the chair. We took one look at the college library, and David Jenkins exclaimed, "What a pity! That's the end! There is nothing that we can do about it!" Subsequent pleas that the staff lent their books to students could not cover up the huge gaps in the library. Our inspection of one of the Jewish colleges set us a similar problem. This time it was another Jewish member who exclaimed, "There's not much that we can do about that!" However, the principal seemed unabashed. He simply asked us when the next inspection could be held, and guaranteed that, if money was the problem, they would purchase a virtually infinite number of books before our next visit! I reflected that it was tragic that our Anglican colleges could not have matched this kind of comment. Much later, when I was a professor at Nottingham, I enjoyed such inspection visits on behalf of the Human Fertilisation and Embryology Authority; then it was a matter not of libraries but of staffing and records. But that is another story, told below.

I have just dug out my diaries for 1975 and 1977. I am utterly appalled! How could I have imagined that I had time to do all those things? Looking at both years, I had about nine or ten hours per week of undergraduate lecturing, plus supervision of around three MA research candidates and one for the PhD. That is quite reasonable for an average lecturing and supervision role. But in addition to this, my timetable was crowded with repeated meetings of the Association of University Teachers, the Non-Professorial Staff Association, preaching at a variety of Sheffield churches, meetings of the Honorary Vice Presidents of the Christian Union, meetings of the Theological Society, regular monthly seminars for post-ordination training, which I led in my area, and student weekends, and almost limitless hospitality. On top of all this, I also attended regular meetings in London, which I have described, as well as speaking engagements at the Universities of Leeds, Exeter, Durham, Oxford, Manchester, and elsewhere.

Further, I had become a member of the Church of England Doctrine Commission, which involved a succession of residential meetings for several days in retreat houses at various locations in the country. In addition to the time spent on meetings, we normally prepared essays and other work for the next meeting.

1977 was a particularly onerous year, because it was the year of the mission to the university, which was sponsored by all the Christian societies, including the Catholic Society and the Christian Union. I had come to function as a liaison officer between the Christian Union and the various chaplaincies. I had also taken on external examining duties in the University of Manchester. As I look through my 1977 engagements, I am amazed at how many meetings of the Mission Committee were deemed apparently necessary, how many post-ordination seminars were held, and how many Theological Society Committee meetings were expected, not to mention meetings of Senate and of the Faculty Boards. Perhaps Church committees are the best way of distracting committed Christians from their primary calling.

The Mission was called "Dialogue 77," to avoid any hint of propaganda or crusade. In practice it was not a misnomer, because we held a month of meetings of genuine dialogue in which such speakers as Trevor Huddleston, Peter Hebblethwaite, Monty Barker, and others from particular disciplines conducted dialogue with Christian faith. The culmination of the month of dialogue meetings was a week of more explicit mission led by Michael Green. I recall his speaking at a meeting in one of the halls of residence in which he asked all those who were not Christians to raise their hand, and when no one responded, he asked the rest of the audience what was the purpose of his and their being there!

The mission was conducted from our home at 53 Westbourne Road, but held in the university. Michael Green often engaged those outside the Christian Union in dialogue and constructive argument in our kitchen. He also showed his capability in mounting a display of convincing chicken noises. Typically he used art and visual aids, including a large wooden cross, for his purposes, and the team of actors. They performed the stories of several parables, often in modern dress, in which one, I remember, involved a butler who delighted the audience by responding to the command, "Here, Thiselton."

When I consider the amount of speaking and preaching engagements that I had accepted and for which I had to prepare, I am not surprised that my first major book appeared as late as 1980. It is a miracle that I had found any time for research at all. Academic articles were a different matter. I remember preparing articles on the parousia, or the return of Christ, on the new hermeneutic, and various other research subjects. Over the years I published some seventy research articles. The supervision, examination, and oral exam of PhD students seemed to cut both ways. On the one hand, they were a fruitful source of suggestive ideas; on the other hand, they undoubtedly took an enormous amount of time.

Indeed, it was the proliferation of articles invited or imposed by publishers that led to the founding of the *Journal for the Study of the Old Testament*. One day, as we were leaving the Senior Common Room together, David Clines remarked to me, "Why are our lives so dictated to by publishers? Why don't we found our own journal, and then write what we like?" Thus began the publication of our two journals JSOT and JSNT, at first with the typewriter and printed in a small room, later printed with justified margin, and finally produced with more professional expertise, to be placed alongside other international journals. This led in turn to two monograph series. For a period I became Review Editor of JSNT. In due course, however, David Clines, David Gunn, and Philip Davies, became main editors of the publications.

Another unusual feature of 1977 was the holding of the, I think, first meeting of the National Evangelical Anglican Congress (NEAC), which happened to be held at Nottingham. As many now know, John Stott had invited me to lecture to the 2000 participants on the subject of hermeneutics. One striking memory was my feeble attempt to use the overhead projector. I remember foolishly exclaiming to the audience, "I don't seem to have the necessary slide"; to which several voices replied, "isn't that it in your hand?" More serious was the clash between John Stott and David Watson about hermeneutics. David Watson seemed to think the subject was a joke, and made comments about "Professor Hermann Neut." John Stott thought that the subject was of the utmost importance. At the final session of the congress, participants were invited to vote on the subject. I was delighted at some 80%–90% voted to take the study of hermeneutics seriously; but disappointed that some 10%–20% consciously abstained from the motion. This would never have happened in America or Germany.

By 1979 I had not only retained all my internal university commitments, but also taken on more external duties and engagements. The bishop of Leicester, then the Rt. Revd. Richard Rutt, had invited me to be his Examining Chaplain. My main duties were to interview those who were about to complete their first year as deacons, when the bishop wanted to assure himself that they were ready to be ordained as priests. This involved asking each candidate about his reading, prayer, and experience of the parish. I was astonished at how greatly these ordained men and women varied. Clearly their greatest embarrassment was when I asked them about reading. There was usually a stunned pause, followed eventually by the comment, "Well, I have been inspired by reading Moltmann."

Within the university I became elected to the Clerical Staff Sub-Committee. We were entrusted with the review of secretarial appointments, and I was amazed to find what differing reports and requests we received from the different faculties of the university. I well remember my colleagues in the Faculty of Arts drawing stunned breath, when a medical professor complained, "My secretary does not even have time to write up my research." For most of us this would have been an impossible dream! It was my first genuine introduction to bureaucracy, because in order to be promoted to a higher grade, there were certain formal hoops through which a secretary would have to go, and these seemed to bear little resemblance to their actual work.

At the same time, my work for Post-Ordination Training continued in Sheffield, and the bishop of Sheffield invited me to lead the ordination retreat. These numerous talks and the ordination sermon again required much preparation. In the same year I was promoted to the rank of Senior Lecturer, and our work under the much loved Professor James Atkinson came to an end with his retirement, and the appointment of Professor John Rogerson in his place. John Rogerson was very conscientious, and deeply concerned with postgraduate research in the department. On the less positive side, he also introduced a multiplicity of staff meetings for us, virtually every week.

It was unfortunate that this huge burden of commitments had led to my being unwell for a period after John Rogerson had arrived. James Atkinson had encouraged me to begin to apply for university chairs. Clearly I did not have quite the same relationship with John Rogerson.

With the encouragement of James Atkinson I did have a stab at the chair of theology in the University of Dublin in February 1980. Indeed, after waiting for what seemed an inordinate elapse of time, I went to Dublin with Rosemary over Easter, to spy out the land. My poor health, however, had extended to suspected angina, and when we learned that the National Health Service did not cover any treatment in Ireland, and that private medicine would not cover pre-existing conditions, we reluctantly concluded that it would be wiser to withdraw the application. I had already met one of the two professors in Dublin, and it left me feeling rather torn up when he commented, "What a shame you withdrew! I'm sure that you would have got it, if you had not withdrawn."

I recall a meeting of the Society for the Study of Theology at which this same academic was dialoguing with another Irishman who had become a professor in Scotland. The latter complained that his one disappointment concerned how many rules and regulations the Scottish universities had. I well remember his Irish reply: "Good gracious! If an Irishman does not know how to bend the rules, nobody can!"

In 1980 I also received an invitation to visit Toronto, and was warmly welcomed. I went in the summer, for I recall many pavement cafés and other attractions. I subsequently told my wife how much she would enjoy Toronto, but we went there in winter, when I found, to my great disappointment, that it had become a quite different city.

John Rogerson had a vision that Sheffield would become a great powerhouse of PhD research and supervision. I certainly supervised my share. Among the early candidates was a British candidate, Clive Garrett, who worked on Bultmann, and a Canadian, Barry Parker, who wrote his dissertation on Paul and the Law. He was often misunderstood, as he described this as "Paul and the Lar." His wife called him "Berry." She was determined to live in an English village, and we drove them round a large number of villages and properties. I was therefore not entirely surprised when he confessed to the major problem of loneliness.

It was otherwise with my other PhD candidates. Stanley Porter came from California, in the first instance to study Reader-Response Theory. But he mistakenly thought that my essay on this subject had pronounced the last word on it. He therefore switched to verbal aspect in *Koinē* Greek. I agreed to supervise him, provided that it would be a joint supervision with Linguistics. He was a prodigious reader, devouring books and articles almost without limit. He is now president, dean, and a professor at McMaster Divinity School in Canada. Stephen Fowl, also from America, now a professor at Loyola University, Maryland, examined the difference between forms and functions in Paul; Jim Routt also came from America to work on Colossians; and other British candidates joined a growing band of research candidates. Porter and Fowl have since produced many publications.

In June 1980 I designed and introduced a university course for teachers who had qualified in other subjects to become qualified in biblical studies, in order to teach in this area. Naturally it was mounted jointly with lecturers in the department and the Faculty of Education. I gained a taste of how genuinely mature students in work wanted to learn, and we held warm, eager, and well-attended classes. The first year we had a bumper attendance, but there were few takers for a second course.

I had begun to feel boxed in by university personnel and concerns, in spite of frequent visits to London for FOAG and other bodies. In October we moved to Fulwood, to 81 Clarendon Road. This was partly for the sake of our children, for them to be within easy reach of the lively church Youth Fellowship. It was partly because our neighbours had changed in Westbourne Road, and owing to their generosity of heart our new next-door neighbours very often acted as host to some dozen children on their back lawn, some disabled, and all very noisy. It did not help my writing.

About this time David Shaw, a former student of Tyndale Hall, Bristol, approached me. He was now vicar of Eyam, the famous mediaeval plague village in Derbyshire. He was pressed by oversight of three churches, and wondered whether I could help at Grindleford, a village about eight miles from Fulwood. In my own parish church, the vicar, Philip Hacking, was in general supportive, but there were less opportunities for ministry than their might have been. Philip made it clear that he viewed academic clergy as "not the front line." At Fulwood, I had seemed to preach seldom, and to preside at Holy Communion, never, to my memory. We therefore agreed to conduct services and preach every Sunday morning. The congregation was friendly and receptive, but usually numbered about twenty-five.

In 1981-82, Calvin College, Grand Rapids, Michigan, invited me to apply for a Professorial Research Fellowship, to work with four American scholars there for one year on hermeneutics. After much heart-searching, Rosemary and I decided that this was worth exploring. If we went, our oldest son, Stephen, could continue work for his "A" levels, while staying with a church family. I was duly interviewed in Grand Rapids, being genuinely open to God's guidance about whether or not we should go there.

In the event I was offered the post, and really enjoyed collaborating with Roger Lundin, Clarence Walhout, and other American colleagues. We enjoyed some wonderful American hospitality and friendship, and have since produced together two books, *The Responsibility of Hermeneutics* (Eerdmans, 1985), and much later, *The Promise of Hermeneutics* (Eerdmans, 1999). For the second book Calvin College paid for Roger Lundin and Clare Walhout to visit me to confer with me in the University of Nottingham. We also found ourselves in the same local church at Grand Rapids as the Senior Editor of Eerdmans, Jon Pott. This became the beginning of a lifetime of friendship. My eldest son, Stephen, came to join us, after he had sat his "A" level exams. I remember his initial comment: "I have never seen you so relaxed, and even wearing an open-neck shirt and no tie!" Stephen and I had a wonderful time for a short break in Toronto.

Conversations in the Theology Faculty Room were often entertaining. I cannot remember the details, but at the time some tension arose about relations with the Canadian Province of Alberta. One American wit suggested, "Why doesn't the USA simply buy Alberta from Canada? That would end the whole thing." I had also hoped to avoid UK restriction on driving because of my eyesight. I therefore underwent driving lessons in Grand Rapids. My first instructor was a charming lady. But when I asked, "What am I to do about the lorry that is bearing down upon us?," she did not address the situation, but only exclaimed, "Gee, a lorry! How cute!! Is that the English word for a truck?"—by which time the crisis was over. I changed instructors to a man, who simply muttered "Illegal!" whenever I dropped below 45 m.p.h. on an expressway. On my return to England, I found that the International Licence—which presented a request for me to be permitted to drive from President Reagan—could not be used.

When we returned to Sheffield, the roads seemed narrow, and the university, good as it was, less friendly and warm, and more formal, than Calvin College. In fact we were seriously considering American and Canadian posts, until (perhaps when I was still in the USA) I happened to see an advertisement for the chair at the University of Exeter. I duly applied for it. The appointment was for 1984.

The omens at the interview, however, were bad. On the interviewing panel was the Exeter professor of philosophy, who bluntly stated in public that only an idiot would have spent time and print on Heidegger. This confirmed the huge gulf between some British departments of philosophy and those in Germany. I should also have been more diplomatic when they asked me about sharing theology with Arabic studies, which would have helped enormously with considerable funding needs. Dr. David Catchpole, whom they eventually appointed, sat at dinner between the vice-chancellor and the external assessor. It was tragic for me that Professor George Caird of Oxford, whom I knew well, and was to be the other assessor, had suddenly died a couple of weeks earlier.

Experiences at Dublin and Exeter had left me feeling profoundly unsettled at Sheffield. I applied for the New Testament chair at Edinburgh University, and was duly shortlisted. Before the interview a very dignified lady took us along some narrow corridors, clearly so that the candidates would not meet one another. The effect was ruined when we reached an intersection, and David Aune, from America, cried out, "Hi, Tony!," in a less than hushed voice. There were fourteen on the Appointing Committee. I learned afterwards that six (plus the vice-chancellor) were from the university, and six from the Church of Scotland, since the university had the charge of training ordinands. I had very gracious exchanges with the university Senate representatives and with the vice-chancellor and with the external assessor, Professor C. F. Evans. It was a pity, however, that another Edinburgh professor had advised me not to be afraid of being transparent about my particular churchmanship. I gathered years afterward that all the academic staff would have appointed me, but the church representatives were not convinced, and ideally wanted a presbyterian. The Appointing Committee in Edinburgh needed a two-thirds majority vote to approve a candidate.

In retrospect it was probably right for me that I was not appointed, and it gave rise to some hilarious jocularity when I returned to have a gall-stones operation, at which both the eminent surgeon and eminent anaesthetist turned out to have applied for Edinburgh chairs, to which neither was appointed.

Edinburgh had led me to think about teaching training ordinands. I had also reached the point where after fifteen years I could almost predict my colleagues' views about everything. Fifteen years seemed the maximum time before being institutionalized creeps in, and I did not want to spend a lifetime in Sheffield. Hence, when St. John's College, Nottingham advertised for a principal, I applied. This was to open a new seven-year chapter of ordination training at two different theological colleges and universities.

Chapter 5

1975–2003

Theological Contributions to, and Recollections of,
The Church of England Doctrine Commission

I WAS STILL AT Sheffield when the archbishops invited me to become a member of the Church of England Doctrine Commission. I served five Commissions, for twenty-eight years. When I joined in 1975 the chairman was the then bishop of Winchester, the Rt. Revd. John Taylor, author of *The Go-Between God*. Looking back, I think that I was able to contribute more on theology than perhaps to any other commission.

The first Doctrine Commission had been appointed by the two archbishops in 1922, and published by SPCK in 1938. It was chaired by Archbishop William Temple, with such members as O. C. Quick, B. H. Streeter, A. E. Rawlinson, and thirteen other members. Its focus included Scripture, the Anglican formularies, the doctrines of God, Christ, and sin, and the church, sacraments, and eschatology. In 1938 *The Times* carried a letter delivering the verdict of the *Catholic Advisory Council*, which then represented 2,000 clergy and 50,000 laity. They criticized it for rejecting miracles and the reality of good and evil spirits, and for treating as "open questions" what Church of England doctrine firmly asserts. It expressed itself "determined to resist to the utmost this threatened disintegration of the Church of England."

The next major report, entitled *Christian Believing*, was published in 1976, again by SPCK. It was chaired by Professor Maurice Wiles of Oxford, with such members as Professor D. E. Nineham, Professor John Macquarrie, and Dr J. I. Packer, alongside fourteen other members. It was not well received by the Church of England as a whole, on the ground that it was better at raising problems than solving them. It declared, "From the very beginning of Christianity there is pluriformity of faith" (p. 28). How could the Bible be anything else, this report asked, "but a collection of many different insights . . . many of them inevitably in tension with one another?" (p. 29) Even if this is technically correct, today numerous qualifying comments would be made to reassure the faithful that the Bible was more than a jumble of contradictory loose ends.

When I joined the Commission in 1975, the public mood was eagerly expecting a more constructive report. The bishop of Winchester was God's man for the hour. Tradition, the bishop argued in his introduction, is not simply about the past: "We see it as a still continuing process of *corporate believing* (p. 2). Expressions of private belief (which featured in the 1976 report) were relative. He pointed to "corporate knowledge" in other disciplines.

Bishop John Taylor held the ring brilliantly between such members as Basil Mitchell, professor of philosophy of religion in the University of Oxford, John Bowker, then professor of religious studies in the University of Lancaster, John Drury, then of the University of Sussex, and W. H. Vanstone, residentiary canon of Chester Cathedral. Virtually all of these became good personal friends over the years.

At the time the bishop of St. Albans also shared the same personal name, "John Taylor," as Winchester's John Taylor. I remember my daughter, Linda, telling me that Bishop John Taylor was to speak at Greenbelt. Assuming that this meant John Taylor of Winchester, I enquired of him about his going to speak at Greenbelt. The bishop was of course mystified and troubled, since the speaker was Bishop John Taylor of St. Albans! He therefore wrote a note to check about this with his chaplain. Of course, I owed him an apology for confusing him with the bishop of St. Albans.

Apart from serious debate, I recall some pithy quips from Basil Mitchell. I was especially entertained as our Commission was located from place to place in diocesan retreat houses, and we were given intricate but extensive information about so-called domestic matters by each warden. Basil Mitchell whispered, "What a massive deluge of useless information!" I was also intrigued by Basil Mitchell's fondness for P. G. Wodehouse's stories about Bertie Wooster and Jeeves. I could not help wondering how many Bertie Woosters he had taught at Oxford.

The most entertaining figure of all was probably Professor John Bowker. Among his postgraduate students was a princess from Thailand. He had many other East Asian contacts, and often arrived early the second or third morning, apologizing that he had received a telegram from a far Eastern student whom he needed to visit, and had therefore spent last night at an elegant and comfortable four-star hotel in the town on his arrival, rather than raising the warden of the retreat house to admit him to more Spartan accommodation at an unearthly hour of the night. On theology, he was such a creative and innovative figure that on his return he would radically reshape the agenda. Above all, it was his stroke of genius to suggest the title for our published report, namely *Believing in the Church: The Corporate Nature of Faith* (SPCK, 1981).

The bishop asked us to write separate chapters, but in critical discussion to make sure that we could genuinely "stand behind" each of the chapters. I was asked to write chapter 3, which I entitled, "Knowledge, Myth, and Corporate Memory." When towards the end, Bishop David Jenkins visited us as Consultant, I was immensely gratified to hear him say: "I suppose chapter 3 is the heart of it all." The first section was on "The corporate foundations of knowledge."

I traced how "wisdom" in the Bible constitutes shared experience and judgments over the centuries, and in philosophy corporate wisdom is defended by Vico and Gadamer, in contrast to the individualism and "knowledge" of Descartes. Archbishop Temple had called Descartes' retreat into solitary contemplation, even if with some exaggeration, as "the most disastrous moment in the history of Europe" (William Temple, *Nature, Man, and God*. Macmillan, 1940, p. 57)!

The transmission of corporate knowledge, I argued, came about through language, but in the church through creeds, sermons, hymns, and reiterations of shared knowledge. Gadamer insists that such belief is above all *reasonable*; far more so than pitting one individual opinion against another. In the church it becomes the transmission of *corporate memory*, inherited from the Bible and apostolic doctrine. In the concluding section the self-contradiction of many uses of the term "myth" was exposed, and I emphatically argued that most uses of this term did more harm than good. In place of myth, I advocated the use of D. D. Evans' term, "self-involvement" or participation.

In the end we produced a book of around 300 pages. Basil Mitchell wrote on "I Believe: We Believe"; Anthony Harvey wrote on Scripture; Tom Wright, John Taylor, and William Vanstone wrote respectively on doctrine declared, implicit, and diffused. John Bowker wrote on religions as systems, in which he carefully examined boundary types in systems of various kinds, including the opposing forces of genotypes and phenotypes, which concerned respectively the continuity of a system or organism and its diversity. John Baker wrote on the development of doctrine. This represents only a sample of the whole book. The report was duly published in 1981.

Over the next five years, until 1986, work towards the report was chaired, first by the bishop of Winchester, and then by the bishop of Salisbury, the Rt. Revd. John Baker. It bore the title *We Believe in God*, and was published by Church House Publishing in 1987. Half a dozen of us survived through from the previous Commission, while Dr. Gareth Bennett, Dr. Sarah Coakley, Dr. John Halliburton, Canon Bill Ind (later bishop of Truro), Colin Buchanan (later bishop of Aston), and Professor Barnabas Lindars, were added to our membership. This time we did not write individual essays, but all of us were involved in every essay.

From the point of view of the Church this may have added to the authority of the report, but from the authors' point of view it meant an extraordinarily demanding attention to wording to which all agreed and in the end led to a smaller report of about hundred and fifty pages.

At the first session Bishop John Baker outlined his hopes for a possible way forward with the next project, and suggested that we all wrote a few notes "on the back of an envelope," which we would present at the next meeting. Those of us who knew the ropes wrote mini-essays, which would take about ten minutes to read through. Colin, however, had taken the bishop literally, and had written half a dozen sentences on the proverbial back of an envelope. When the bishop invited him to speak, he began with the typically memorable words, "I feel like a man exposed in his underclothes!" Colin was deeply disappointed not to have been reappointed to the Liturgical Commission, and stated publicly that to be on the Doctrine Commission was a very poor consolation prize.

We addressed challenges to believing in God, the reliability of knowledge, faith, and certainty, and the language of the imagination, including poetry. A separate chapter was devoted to the God of the Bible, the God of Jesus, and the God of the disciples. One of the most important chapters was entitled "God as Trinity: An Approach through Prayer." Much of the inspiration for this chapter came from Dr. (now professor) Sarah Coakley, who stressed the role of the Holy Spirit in articulating prayer to God in Romans 8:26. This means that we can be "Caught up in a divine conversation, passing back and forth in and through the one who prays," while "the Spirit himself bears witness with our spirit" (Rom 8:16; p. 108).

Bill Vanstone and John Taylor shared a concern to portray the vulnerability of God, who was in some ways, constrained by the materials through which he acted on humankind, and worked on the world. They suggested the analogy of an artist whose repertoire is not unlimited, because of the constraints of the material with which he works. On the other hand, two of our consultants were Rt. Revd. Kenneth Cragg, assistant bishop in Jerusalem, and Dr. Herbert McCabe, of the Dominican Order of Blackfriars in Oxford, and both were keen to stress, by contrast, the transcendence of God.

The third session that I recall, from 1986 to 1989, was chaired initially by the bishop of Salisbury, but he was advised in 1987 by his doctor that he should either resign from the House of Lords or resign the chairmanship of the doctrine commission for reasons of poor health. In a farewell meeting, he reflected on his life, commenting that when he was canon of Westminster Abbey his duties were so time-consuming and varied as to make theological research and writing extremely difficult, if not impossible. During that time, he published *The Foolishness of God*, but in effect nothing else. Ironically the archbishop of Canterbury had urged him to accept this job, on the ground that it would give him more time for theological research than his Oxbridge academic post. Sadly, I have heard of such events many times. The Church of England will not give adequate time for research.

When John was bishop of Salisbury, his chaplain, John Meacham, reported to us that often he did not reach home until the small hours from the House of Lords, in which he was a conscientious and studious attender and participant. He therefore resigned from the Commission in 1987, and I was appointed for six months as caretaker chairman, until the bishop of Newcastle, the Rt. Revd. Alec Graham, became free to chair the meeting.

One of my early experiences of this Commission, which in this one respect was less than happy, came during one of the first chapel services. It appeared that we had no pianist or organist to play the hymns. Ruth Etchells was ever the cheerful optimist. With eyes steadfastly looking at the ground, I heard Ruth exclaim to everyone, "Anthony would absolutely *love* to play." No disclaimer from me was accepted.

Dr. Coakley and I had remained members from the previous Commission. But many new members joined us, including Professor David Brown, Canon Derek Stanesby, and Professor Rowan Williams. Several other members joined us in 1989 including Dr. John Polkinghorne. The subject was that of the Holy Spirit. I recall one impasse. This was when a female member threatened to resign if the Holy Spirit were not described as "She"; upon which a male canon threatened to resign if the Holy Spirit were not called "He"! Our poor Bishop John, as chairman, spent hours writing numerous paragraphs with gender-free pronouns, including such reflexive pronouns as "Gods-self!"

The bishop of Newcastle, Alec Graham, was great fun. Bishop Alec loved dogs and train-spotting. On one occasion his Archdeacon was not free to look after his dog, Zilla, and Zilla came to lie under the table while we engaged in serious theological debate. Our self-deprecating secretary, John Meacham, sent an article to the *Church Times* on our work, which they published. He entitled it: "Blond Bombshell Helps Doctrine Commission." Only at the very end of his article were readers informed that the "blond bombshell" was none other than Zilla, the bishop's dog. On one occasion Ruth Etchells also brought her dog. As the dogs chased each other round the table, Sarah Coakley was heard to mutter, "They never would have allowed this if it was babies!"

Bishop Alec was extraordinarily warm and friendly, and full of gloriously eccentric anecdotes. For example, he admitted to addressing clergy sometimes through his dog, especially when things grew tricky. When he was presented in his work as bishop with a tricky pastoral problem he would dialogue: "Well, now, Zilla (his dog), what shall we do? He should not really have pocketed all that money, should he?" In real life, when we waited on a railway platform, he at once held dialogue with the boys who also collected train numbers.

To match earlier reports, we entitled this one *I Believe in the Holy Spirit* (1991). On "charismatic experience," insights were solid rather than epoch-making. We included the notion of speaking in tongues as "releasing the unconscious" (p. 27), and contrasted scholastic and Pietist approaches. The church fathers were quoted, but we also included contemporary "interviews." We noted the possibility of depression and mood swings if the "charismatic" aspect were overemphasized.

The chapter entitled "This Is That" went further. It compared puzzles in Acts with Old Testament and Christocentric perspectives. Unlike the later Healing Report (discussed in the chapter on the Synod), we showed more caution about "certainty" of healing (p. 52). We concluded, "Openness to change, vitality, warmth, and surprise, all need to be balanced by continuity, regularity, stability, and rationality" (p. 55). We stressed the Christocentric nature of the work of the Spirit: "Jesus is a 'Spirit-filled' human being" (p. 64). We wrote of the Trinity: "God is an everlasting movement of giving away" (p. 67). We discussed the Spirit of Power and the Spirit of Truth, the Spirit and Creation, and the Spirit and the Future.

When the report appeared, some criticized it for not being "biblical." Bishop Alec was dismayed and indignant. After all, there were well over 200 biblical references in the index!

Our previous chairman, Bishop Alec, continued as chair, and our next report was called *The Mystery of Salvation* (1995). Four of us remained as continuing members. We were joined by Professor Richard Bauckham, Dr. Christina Baxter, Lady (Sophie) Laws, and again by Tom Wright, at that time dean of Lichfield Cathedral. We now had six diocesan bishops: Geoffrey Rowell, Rowan Williams, John Taylor, Peter Selby, and Stephen Sykes, formerly Regius Professor at Cambridge, and Alec Graham.

An introduction rightly considered what we are saved *from*, and what we are saved *to*. Anglicans do hold specific beliefs about this. However, we must also take into account contemporary issues, such as that of the sciences, polemical critiques, and our relation to other faiths. The second chapter, "The Giver and the Gift," stressed that there could often be too much talk about *gifts* with relatively little talk about the *Giver*. The greatest gift from God is *God's own self*. A third chapter, on "Saving History," discussed telling the Christian story, while a fifth chapter discussed retelling the story today. The Old Testament constitutes a vital background, and thus we asserted: "Sacrifice seems to involve a transaction or exchange, and this is taken up in the familiar New Testament equation 'the just for the unjust'" (1 Pet 3:18; p. 116).

In the final chapter, "Ending the Story," I succeeded in inserting one of my hobbyhorses, namely that heaven is *not simply static perfection*, but is *ever new, ongoing participation in the life of the living God*; a crescendo rather than a static fortissimo (p. 196). We also considered the question of universalism and the reality of hell. We quoted John Burnaby's words, "Dogmatic universalism contradicts the very nature of love.... Love cannot, because it will not, compel the surrender of a single heart that holds out against it.... Love never forces" (p. 198). Hence: "Final judgement, therefore remains a reality, although Hell is not eternal torment, but it is final, and an irrevocable choosing of that which is opposed to God so completely and so absolutely that the only end is total nonbeing" (p. 199).

I was finally involved in a fifth Report: *Being Human: The Christian Understanding of Personhood, Illustrated with Reference to Power, Money,*

Sex and Time (Church House Publishing, 2003). Our chairman for my fifth term was Bishop Stephen Sykes. This time we amounted to sixteen members. We were joined by Professor David Ford, Regius Professor of Divinity at Cambridge, Dr. Alistair McFadyen of Leeds, Professor Michael Banner of Kings College, London, Bishop Kenneth Stevenson, bishop of Portsmouth, and several others. Stephen Sykes wanted this report to be practical, and hence suggested that it should address the use of power, money, sex, and time, from a Christian and Anglican point of view. After an initial chapter on Scripture, we addressed these areas.

On *power*, we argued that Christians are participants in the divine nature, and that God's power does not involve the use of brute force, even if it could also act with authority. Indeed the power of the cross was very different from the secular or worldly notions of power, and power could be manifested in weakness, as Paul commented, especially in 1 Corinthians 1–2.

On *money* we declared: "Money is not the problem. . . . We are the problem. It is not money that defines us . . . , but our personal *attitudes*" (p. 57). Money may be a "good," which enables the development and flourishing of human communities, but the market in money can cause great harm. Bishop Peter Selby particularly stressed the broken link between money and reality, and the dangers of a money market which overestimated its real value, by letting money on paper chase money on paper. In many ways he anticipated the dangers of the 2008–9 crash.

We addressed changing patterns of *sexual relations*, stressing that 1 Corinthians 7:1, "It is well for a man not to touch a woman," constitutes the "quotation of a slogan misused at Corinth" (p. 81). Love, we stressed, reflects the love of God for us. We commented,

> God desires and accepts love as well as giving it. God chooses not to be self-contained, but deeply involved with others whom God has made to be his partners in the world. God is pained by rejection and abuses of his love, and God's love impels him towards overcoming obstacles and damage to the relationship of love that God intends to have with human beings. (p. 85).

We added, "Sexual engagement is mutually involving. It entails give-and-take, desire and delight, loss of control, and self surrender" (p. 86). Above all, it seeks the good of the other person. We recognized, however, that it could go terribly wrong, and cause agony and misery. We acknowledged that sexual union can seem disappointing in relation to the expectations of fantasy. We also expressed reservations about social constructionism.

On *time*, we recognized that God gives world time in and with the creation itself. We examined the theories by Stephen Hawking and others. We stressed the needs for patience, citing the example that trees take years to grow into their full stature. We recognized that time gives scope for patience and faithfulness. But there are many ways of construing and understanding time, for which we cited examples from literature, science, and music.

This session of the doctrine commission was also full of fun. Alistair McFadyen was particularly gifted in unexpectedly seizing the bishop's chair for himself, and in promoting numerous other pieces of acceptable mischief. By 2003, however, I was compelled to retire from my professorship at Nottingham, and from the Synod, and hence I resigned from the Doctrine Commission. I sorely missed the companionship and friendship, but found that I could use the time much more fruitfully by pursuing my own work!

Chapter 6

1985–92

College and University in Nottingham and Durham

My interview at St. John's Theological College, Nottingham, brought several surprises. I knew the chairman of council, Bishop Roy Williamson, and had every confidence in his leadership. I had met several of the staff. I knew that the university would be likely to appoint me as a Special Lecturer, if I was appointed to the principalship of the college. My course on hermeneutics was therefore probably assured. I did not know much more about the college and its administration, except that it was flourishing.

My initial shock came on visiting the college chapel. It was a modern building, shaped in the form of a plain rectangle on its side, with one minor gesture to tradition. This was one small stained-glass window. It accentuated, rather, the modernity of the rest of the "room." My second shock came when I went to investigate the organ, and found that in place of the normal organ, there was a drum kit and space for a band. This at once made me feel uneasy, and I suggested to Rosemary that perhaps we were in the wrong place, and should return home.

The irony was increased when I discovered several years later that one of the four shortlisted applicants, namely Tom Wright, had experienced the same misgivings. But whereas Tom had said to his wife, "It can't be too bad if Anthony Thiselton has applied," I had said to Rosemary, "It can't be too bad if Tom Wright has applied." In the event I think that we both had a happy interview with the teaching staff, and I was reassured that the bursar or finance officer was an ex-manager of a Barclays Bank, who had his hand firmly on the finances.

In the event, Roy Williamson, as chairman, offered me the post. My visit to Edinburgh had set me thinking about the pastoral oversight of ordinands, and St. John's would constitute a far closer community than I had experienced in the Department at Sheffield. I gathered that I would retain some university profile as Special Lecturer at the university. The college was flourishing with about ninety students. I therefore accepted the appointment. But the sting was in the tail. Bishop Roy Williamson then told me that he was on the brink of resigning as chairman of council, and that it had been virtually agreed to appoint Mrs Gloria Rich as chairman of council. Her experience as a layperson was in the field of education, and I did not know her at all.

My period of preparation for St. John's now began. Professor Geoffrey Sims, the vice-chancellor of Sheffield University, expressed his horror and disappointment at my leaving, hinting at what the future might have held. But I had a nice letter from the lay Chaplain of St. John's, Felicity Lawson, asking what music I would like to choose for the inaugural service. One piece of music that I had always treasured was Stanford's *Te Deum* in B flat. I therefore asked for this. Felicity Lawson replied that she did not think the college could run to this, but would be able to offer a range of songs.

I arrived at the college full of hope, but soon discovered that the college staff and most of the students regarded themselves as a flagship of the charismatic movement in the Church of England. I had indeed been asked at the interview whether I felt positively about the charismatic movement, and had given a guarded but mildly and cautiously positive reply. I did indeed value its apparent thirst for intimacy with God and spiritual renewal. I had not, however, bargained for how extreme, in my judgement, the charismatic element was. I never fully enjoyed chapel worship while I was there. I asked one ordinand what had been his highlight at St. John's, to which he replied, "Learning to play the drums!" St. John's and many of its students were a whole different world away from what I knew or was expecting!

I was looking forward to both teaching and pastoral work, but found that pastoral one-to-one interviews were far more time-consuming than teaching. I had not expected that Frank Lake's connection with Nottingham would still linger on. Lake (1914–82) had been a clinical psychotherapist at Nottingham and had founded the Clinical Theology Association, which was influential in the 1960s, 1970s, and early 1980s, and made much of the "clinical" approach to pastoral counselling, including "the healing of memories." I had not realized that staff and students would still be talking about this theory. No one seemed aware of the books by Donald Capps and others, which argued for the need to abandon the old "therapeutic" or healing model of pastoral counselling in exchange for a "hermeneutical" one, i.e., one that focused on mutual understanding, and on probing beneath the surface text in which those being counselled explained their anxieties or problems, to discover a deeper subtext beneath it. I spent hours with some students who had been abused in childhood, and had problems for which I was unprepared. Gordon Oliver, Director of Pastoral Studies, taught students to understand themselves as "wounded healers."

A number of students, however, were very able, intelligent, and competent, and appreciated genuine theology and training of the Christian mind. Many in those days studied for the University of Nottingham BA or BTh. The mixing with university students and others from Lincoln Theological College was healthy for all concerned. St. John's College also had (and still has) probably the finest theological library of all theological colleges in England, and one of my most gratifying and enjoyable times was gaining and using money for the library from Nottingham Council for an extended library project, which entailed employing several part-time helpers and a project manager.

I fell into trouble on almost the first week when I was due to preach. I had always expected that hymns would be chosen in order to match the message of the sermon. I did not realize that some students had waited for a very long time until the moment when they had the privilege of choosing their favourite "hymn." When, therefore, I attempted to choose a hymn which fitted the sermon, there followed outrage and floods of tears, and the message that the new principal was authoritarian and insensitive.

I had mistakenly assumed that the theological college could serve in England as a mini-university with the addition of pastoral training, even if, unlike the American scene, it could never compete with the level of research undertaken in universities. I did indeed expect that a proportion of the staff, even if a minority, would major on pastoral, practical, day-to-day issues. But at St. John's only a relatively small proportion of the staff seemed interested in pursuing long-term research goals.

Whereas I had begun with a vision for the college, I felt that it was virtually impossible to implement it. With expectations that all staff had an equal vote on introducing new ideas or emphases, I knew that I was powerless to influence the juggernaut! In my view, the college had tended to become somewhat inbred; a view shared by a subsequent Bishop of Southwell and Nottingham.

Nevertheless, I found time to continue some external engagements. The most demanding was probably the Theological Board of Studies of the Council for National Academic Awards (CNAA), which involved many ground-level inspections of many colleges and polytechnics. I also belonged to the CNAA Committee of Arts and Humanities. I participated in the Doctrine Commission, Church of England working parties on theological courses, FOAG, Women Deacons, Anvil Trust, and related matters, and served on the East Midlands Training Course Council. The college also had a plentiful supply of visiting speakers, who included Professor Tom Torrance and others. I visited America as visiting professor in theology at Fuller Theological Seminary, Pasadena, California.

When Ruth Etchells, principal of St. John's, Durham, approached me with the possibility of applying for the post of principal there, it seemed as if my dream of ordination training might come true. This college was uniquely both a full university college and a college with an Anglican theological training college within it. In the event, I applied for the principalship. My interview with the Council of St. John's, Durham, was very different from that of St. John's, Nottingham. My first question at the interview was how I would react to a student who wanted to enjoy himself or herself, rather than work. I remember replying that I had not regarded enjoying oneself and working as exclusive alternatives. I then set out layers of strategy depending on whether this was the first or a persistent offence.

The teaching and administrative staff in St. John's, Durham, gave immense support. The college employed about sixty staff in all, and housed about 360 students. The college contained two halls: St. John's Hall, for university students in all disciplines, and Cranmer Hall, for Anglican ordinands. There was good interchange between the two halls, and informally they often operated as a helpful but informal marriage bureau. The chapel was a lovely, ancient, former parish church, within yards of Durham Cathedral. My only regret was that our youngest son, Martin, had already been offered a place to read Music at St. John's College, Durham, but it now seemed more appropriate for him to be transferred to the College of St. Hild and St. Bede, Durham, where, incidentally he was very happy, and regularly played the organ. He was also director of "Fiddler on the Roof" for enthusiastic student audiences.

The three college officers, in addition to the principal, were the Senior Tutor of St. John's Hall, namely Dr. Peter Forster, later bishop of Chester; the Warden of Cranmer Hall, Rev. Ian Cundy, later bishop of Peterborough; and the bursar, a former major. The four college officers together made most management decisions, even if decisions were the ultimate responsibility of the principal. I recall walking down South Bailey with Peter Forster and Ian Cundy, and hearing one of the women students remark, "The triumvirate!" Ruth Etchells had made all appointment committees "advisory" to the principal, in contrast to St. John's Nottingham, where a straight majority vote among the academic staff determined the matter. On some matters I could even become a liberalizing and progressive force at Durham!

We held all major celebrations in Durham Cathedral. Hence, on my arrival, I felt able to ask once again for Stanford's *Te Deum* in B flat. This time it was performed magnificently by the college choir, and was a complete delight. Bishop David Jenkins also preached the sermon at my licensing, and we had already become firm friends in our work together for the CNAA. This was only slightly spoilt by a fault in the amplification of the Cathedral (provided by the university), which left some of his incisive humour unheard.

Ruth Etchells had strongly recommended that I taught a course on spirituality, which for me was the first time for this subject. As at St. John's, Nottingham, I did find that my teaching did not always play to my strengths. Moreover, the Department of Theology in Durham asked me to lecture, for example, on the literary criticism of the Synoptic Gospels, which I had done many times before at Sheffield. But this was not my primary field of expertise, and I did not regard it as especially exciting or immediately relevant to those who were ordinands. This particular course involved a close comparison of the similarities and differences between the Synoptic Gospels. But if it had been my choice, I should have chosen to teach the *theology* of the Gospels, not literary comparisons between them!

Examining in the university was usually enjoyable, but for me involved one small disadvantage. I was asked to conduct an oral Greek exam for those who had not reached a given standard in the subject. In those days a certain standard in Greek had to be reached before a student could be awarded an honours degree. I did my best to help the candidates.

I fed them easy Greek sentences, such as, "Jesus led the disciples into the wilderness." Imagine my surprise, therefore, when on leaving the Exam Hall, I heard one of the students exclaim in disgust, "The examiner only wants us to sweat."

Otherwise examining was enjoyable, especially since Cranmer students almost always performed very well indeed and several earned first-class degrees. One of our ordinands, Dr. Andrew Colby, had already been a lecturer at Leicester University, and was being scrutinized for a first class degree. One of the younger staff raised objections to such an award. Professor Edward Hulmes leaned over to me, and said in a stage whisper, "What can you do when a man with a second-class mind wants to deprive a man with a first-class mind of a first-class degree?" We awarded him his well-deserved First. I had good relations with the student body at Durham University. For example, I served on the Joint Committee of the University and Students Union. I also carried all my many external appointments with me, and added some extras, such as conducting the Durham Ordination Retreat.

At one point, all the twelve Colleges except ours went on strike over fees. The difference at St. John's was that I had invited the student officers to scrutinize our account books. On this basis I could ask them, "If you want your fees lowered, who do you think should suffer: the washing up and serving ladies; the academic staff; the accounts staff, groundsmen, decorators, fund-raisers, or who else? They all agreed that in this light the fees were reasonable, and made a unanimous recommendation to the students not to strike, even at the risk of criticism from students of other colleges.

The University Senate was even more enjoyable than the Senate at Sheffield. The Senate itself decided to whom to award honorary degrees, and the vice-chancellor, Dr. Evelyn Ebsworth, always urged the need for strict confidentiality. The fiercest debate that I recall involved a redoubtable lady professor in archaeology, who in the midst of her debate with a fellow professor offered to take him outside and "give him a bloody nose if he did not agree." A close second for fierceness concerned the use of computers. The dean of Science, if I remember correctly, was advocating using PC and Windows; the professor of computing science advocated equally firmly the use of Apple-Macintosh. Again, if I remember correctly, members of the Department of Theology were equally divided between the two types of computer.

Ruth Etchells had urged me that the two things needed by a college principal was another principal with whom to share burdens and decisions about the college, and a bolt hole in which to escape. The first was easy to find: Dr. Judy Turner, principal of Van Mildert College, proved herself to be a wise and level-headed confidante, who was also a committed Christian. Both of us, together with Dr. Gerald Blake, the principal of Collingwood College, restrained the other principals from encouraging a pub crawl round Durham and its twelve colleges during the first week of term.

It took more time to find a suitable bolt hole, but we eventually purchased an ex-council house on the coast at Marsden, which looked out onto the sea. While we were occupying this house, the Great North Run went close by the seaside fence of our back garden. This proved to be an occasion to share a picnic with a neighbour, and to get to know a number of the locals. We loved the coast at Marsden.

A fortnightly cycle of duties worked well, in which the first Sunday I would officiate at the Cathedral and preside at lunch, with members of the senior common room. On alternate Sundays Dr. Peter Forster, the Senior Tutor, would preside at lunch and attend his Durham church, while we escaped to our bolt-hole in Marsden. Durham took processions very seriously. One example is that of the Cathedral annual Service of Founders and Benefactors. The bishop, dean, and canon theologian would recite the unpronounceable names of mediaeval benefactors, and the whole congregation would then process to the Chapel of St. Cuthbert. Peter Forster once memorably described this as a combination of solemn Mass and Gilbert and Sullivan.

The college principals were an integral part of the university community. In the university processions we normally stood together, with our names called out in a fixed order by the beadle (the one whose job was to marshal and lead ceremonial processions), entering the degree-awarding ceremony in the castle behind other senators. Unlike most civic universities, the university procession would then proceed into the cathedral for worship and prayer, while the few who did not regard it appropriate to hold a service in the cathedral would then peel off to private occupations.

The twelve principals met regularly together to discuss matters of mutual interest. One of the more memorable meetings concerned preparation to meet the vice-chancellor as heads of houses. Dr. David Jasper, principal of St. Chad's College, was absent. We had discussed interviewing applicants to the university in conjunction with departments. Most of us believed that this was vital to maintaining the distinctive ethos of each college. A minority, including David Jasper, preferred to use the time for research. Our chairman, Dr. Vernon Armitage, principal of Hild and Bede, recommended *not* raising this with the vice-chancellor, since we were divided. When we met the vice-chancellor, David Jasper, against our consensus, asked to be relieved of interviewing prospective students! A mild storm arose in the meeting; but it was nothing compared with after the vice-chancellor's departure. I had always imagined that "handbagging" someone was metaphorical. But as soon as the coast was clear, the principal of our all-women's college proceeded to use her handbag literally as a weapon with which to vent her wrath on David Jasper.

On a similar subject, there was a time of friction in Durham between town and gown, especially between youths from the town and students in pubs. The vice-chancellor was concerned to prove to the City that the colleges brought great benefits to them. So he asked the colleges for a list of what they offered. St. John's students gave me an impressive list. It included prison visiting; taking children from deprived areas on holiday in the country or to the sea; obviously staffing local youth clubs and churches; raising funds for the deprived in Durham and overseas; and at least a dozen substatial other things. At Senate the vice-chancellor reported that only one college, namely St. John's, had given him the kind of list that he had expected, and asked why that was the case. It was one of my proudest moments. It showed everyone what it meant to be a Christian college in action!

Another moment of privilege was when I realized that over some three years we had a bumper batch of very able students. These included the present archbishop of Canterbury, Justin Welby, as well as his present chaplain, Jo Bailey (now Jo Bailey-Wells, wife of Dr. Sam Wells, vicar of St. Martin in the Fields). Justin Welby was always a ready source of advice to me, as well as a most effective pastoral presence among students of both halls. A crisis emerged when we learned that the Treasurer of the Cranmer Hall Common Room had been persuaded to sign an agreement for a photocopier, which, unbeknown to him, technically made him liable for a payment of £200,000, which was a huge sum in around 1990 (the equivalent of £434,400/$695,500 in 2014).

1985-92

Within St. John's College, one hall, Cranmer Hall, was for ordinands. In 1992 we benefitted from some extraordinarily able ordinands. This picture of Cranmer Hall ordinands shows Archbishop (later) Justin Welby (left end of front row); behind him is (later) Archdeacon Jan McFarlane, and behind tutor Dr. Longenecker, Jo Bailey (now Jo Bailey-Wells), chaplain to the archbishop of Canterbury.

Justin Welby, who had been Treasurer of Enterprise Oil in the City of London, strongly recommended that I kept aloof from this, in case the photocopy company decided to sue the college for the money. He then proceeded to lobby newspapers, journalists, MPs, and others about the plight of the Student Common Room. Eventually the turning-point came when he contacted the *Watchdog*, the BBC consumer programme, who photographed the "few bits of furniture which the ordinands owned," and the company then pre-empted the broadcast by saying that it had all been mistake.

My part had been minimal. Several Durham colleges had been similarly caught. So I phoned Dr. Vernon Armitage, principal of Hild and Bede, making the initial comment, "I believe that Hild and Bede are in the same boat." "Not quite," he replied. He added, "Our students tried to see how fast the photocopier could go when the students pushed it down Leaze Hill; I don't suppose yours did!" I also phoned the bishop of St. Alban's, as was our duty as principals of theological training colleges, to say that one of his potential curates was in possible trouble, with the threat to demand a debt of £200,000 hanging over him. The bishop was very calm. "Well," he said, "It makes a change from threats about adultery, I suppose!" Another victim was the Archdeaconry of Northumbria. The Archdeacon's response, however, verged on panic. "We must be very careful," he warned me over the phone, "they are threatening stern legal action!"

Before the graduation ceremonies there was often a line of students to see me. It was a Durham regulation and everyone had to clear the bills before they were allowed to graduate. Many came with excuses, including the standard comment, "My father would be furious if I do not graduate, but I cannot pay my bill." This often called for a reminder about the amount of money spent on beer and the account with the college bar, and to ask whether such an amount was strictly necessary. Occasionally this was combined with an indulgence to pay by instalments if the college could be fairly certain of recouping the money in due course. I had to steer a middle course between the severity of the bursar's office and the precedent of Ruth Etchell's instalment arrangements, the validity and wisdom of which were often doubted by the bursar.

During one year the theological college principals and senior staff received an invitation to share with other theological college staff in a visit to Israel. It would be a winter visit, and I was very grateful that I had taken warm clothes. Part of the itinerary was an audience with one of the Armenian bishops in Jerusalem. At the time our lecturer in Old Testament was Bob Fyall, a Presbyterian, who made no secret of his regarding this projected visit as far from the best use of time. In a distinct Scottish accent he would lament, "Why could we no' see Megiddo instead?" We duly met the bishop, who spoke with deep Christian devotion, passion, and sincerity. Bob Fyall now viewed things utterly differently. In a hushed Scottish accent he would breathe, "Ah! What a gawdly Mon!"

In many ways we could have stayed at Durham for many years. Professor James Dunn, Professor Dan Hardy, Dr. Alan Ford, and Dr. Walter Moberly were four of many in the Department of Theology who made me very welcome. In several cases they belonged to our Senior Common Room. Professor Dunn regularly participated in our weekly meetings, and also became president of the Senior Common Room, which took on a high profile when we welcomed visitors at dinner. I recall that on one such occasion we had just appointed a new catering manager. One of the college principals, Dr. Daphne Levine, observed that a college could run without a principal, but never without a catering manager.

I had two wonderful PAs, first Mrs. Doreen Ayling, and then Mrs. Aileen Jones. Mrs. Ayling lived in the flat above my study, and was tireless in assisting me with my needs. I well recall that after she had prepared the best room in the college, called the Tristram Room, in such a way as to be wholly appropriate to the Bishop's Council, some of the students had ransacked the room, and purloined some items from it. Mrs. Ayling rose at 6:30 a.m., and went round to the rooms of known culprits, and battered on their doors. She reclaimed purloined property, and by 9 a.m. the Tristram Room was immaculate and ready for the bishop.

Mrs. Aileen Jones was also invaluable, not least because she had earlier worked as secretary to the university registrar. Many of her former colleagues remembered her, and she was able to gain advance intelligence of many items of university policy. Both PAs were adept at giving the impression that to be interviewed by the principal could be terrifying (which it was not), and that it would be wiser to see the senior tutor. In fact, Dr. Forster was excellent at maintaining discipline, and this also helped to ease my workload.

Our small house in Marsden was a great asset. In one study-leave period, I wrote a large proportion of *New Horizons in Hermeneutics: The Theory and Practice of Transforming Biblical Reading* (Harper-Collins, 1992). I had begun it during a period in Israel, when owing to a bus strike, I discovered the superb library resources at the Ecumenical Institute in Tantur, on the West Bank, but just outside Jerusalem. That was our first visit to Israel, when Rosemary accompanied me, and we discovered the wonders of Galilee, Jerusalem, Bethlehem, and elsewhere. The fellowship at Tantur was warm and unforgettable.

One of the less easy parts of the job was the necessity of raising money. I quickly discovered that appeals to local churches often brought in a cheque for £10 or £20, with a request that the principal would visit the church to preach. On the other hand, letters to trusts either produced nothing or a cheque for £10,000 or more. I enjoyed the advice of a wonderful Christian stockbroker from Newcastle, who later chaired our Crown Nomination Commission for the appointment of one of our archbishops. This agenda of fundraising came to a head when I toured a number of sites with Peter Forster and Ian Cundy to purchase and build on a second site in Durham. This eventually turned out well, but not without endless work, planning, and anxiety.

When the University of Nottingham advertised an appointment to its chair of Christian theology, this appointment seemed extraordinarily inviting. I could return to research and writing without all the daily distractions of college life. I was a great admirer of Professor Alan Richardson, who had been Nottingham's professor of Christian theology in about 1960, and I knew from my previous knowledge of the department that its scheme of courses and lectures was exactly my ideal. In many ways it was a similar department to Durham, even if on a smaller scale. I therefore duly made application for the appointment, and was delighted to be shortlisted. This was just in time to present reviews and commendations of *New Horizons in Hermeneutics*.

Award of Durham University DD in 1993, for published work

Chapter 7

1992−2002

The Nottingham Chair of Christian Theology

ON THE DAY OF my interview, everything worked out well. I first met some members of the department informally, and then met the dean and some members of Senate. I had two formal interviews: the first was with the vice-chancellor; the second, with the Appointing Committee, mainly from Senate. Sir Colin Campbell was most impressive. He informed me that he could have had a relatively easy time at Nottingham, if he were happy for Nottingham University to coast along in the middle rank of universities. However, it was his aim and ambition that Nottingham University should always feature among the first six universities in England, and he would welcome potential professors who are willing to work hard to achieve the same end. This suited me down to the ground, for it reflected my own aim for the department.

My second and main normal interview was with members of Senate. The questions and concerns matched my own. The professor of philosophy, Bob Kirk, asked me several careful questions about Wittgenstein. He noticed that my published work had included research on this philosopher. He first asked me in general what theologians might gain from Wittgenstein's work. I answered that perhaps most important of all was the close link between language and life, including practical behaviour in life which could lend credibility to words and utterances. I then suggested, second, that conceptual analysis was important and illuminating. I selected Wittgenstein's famous example of the difference between love and pain. I imagined someone's saying, "Ouch! That really hurt!—Oh, it's all right; it's gone off now!" I then contrasted this with another person's saying, "I love you dearly—Oh, it's all right; it's gone off now!" Love is neither an emotion nor a sensation. I compared the conceptual grammar of the respective replies. Would the same reaction to expressions of love and pain make sense? Everyone laughed, and saw the point.

The two external assessors were Professor Henry Chadwick, K.B.E., Master of Peterhouse, Cambridge, and formerly Regius Professor of Divinity at Cambridge, and Professor John Mahony, a Roman Catholic professor of ethics at London. Both, I think, treated me very well, and let me off lightly. The other two short-listed candidates were a Catholic regent master and a Methodist professor. One of the candidates arrived frustrated, because he had bought first-class tickets to travel to Nottingham, but his trains did not offer first class seats!

I had to travel back to Durham without knowing the outcome, but I was shortly phoned by the registrar to offer me the post, which I accepted with delight. The next requirement was to find appropriate accommodation in Nottingham. Initially we selected fourteen properties from a list compiled from estate agents. On arrival we found twelve of them to be unacceptable, and phoned some from a coin box to decline to view the houses. Of the two remaining houses, one had an irritating barking dog next door. Rosemary pointed out that if I was irritated after ten minutes, I would be out of my mind if we lived there permanently. In any case this house would have entailed an upstairs study, and a long walk to the nearest shops. So we declined with thanks.

The fourteenth house was an answer to all our prayers. It was built in about 1790, but had wrongly been advertised as a Victorian property. To our delight, it had remained on the property market for several months, as it was probably rather overpriced. In the event the owners had reduced the price, and we gladly made the purchase, even though we knew that much work would need to be done on the property. In retrospect the work was terrifying, but well worth doing. After twenty-two years in Nottingham, I have never seen a house and gardens that I should have preferred.

When we first drew up to the house, I remember Rosemary's saying, "The Chemist is only the other side of the road; that will do you fine!" More to the point, we knew Attenborough Church nearby from our previous time in Nottingham, and St. Mary's, Attenborough, was our idea of an ideal church. The preaching was biblical; it was a CPAS parish; and there was also a robed choir often with traditional services, which combined Common Worship on Sunday mornings with the Book of Common Prayer on Sunday evenings. We have enjoyed both the house and the church for twenty-two years to date. The house allows for a large ground-floor study, and when I lost my study in the university, it allowed for our dry-proofing an outhouse for use as a book room. It had a very pleasant large and mature garden, both the front and especially at the back.

Our large back garden in Nottingham, with Rosemary (primary gardener) and me

Anthony and Rosemary in the garden

Nottingham University has a beautiful landscaped campus, and normally guarantees accommodation in student halls. It is not surprising that it is one of the most highly-subscribed in the country. During my first day in the university, I was welcomed by the professor of Russian, Professor Malcolm Jones, with great warmth and kindness. I already knew some of the classics staff, who had recently moved from the University of Sheffield. I would soon come to know well all the professors in the Faculty of Arts. My inaugural lecture would come about a year later, and by this time I would have been awarded the DD from the University of Durham. The appointment gave great pleasure to Professor Atkinson, who had long been my mentor.

The Department of Theology was located in the Trent Building, which was the main hub or central building of the whole university, close to the library and Senior Common Room Club. My secretary, Mrs. Mary Elmer, occupied the room adjacent to mine, which enjoyed an adjoining door. Thereby I could lock the door between the main corridor and my room, and any visitor would have to arrange with Mrs. Mary Elmer to see me. It was a grand room, perhaps 20' x 20', and I had bookshelves round the walls from floor to ceiling. I bought a circular table for tutorials, and had the delight of holding them in my room. The teaching staff of the department had rooms on the same corridor.

In addition to coming to know colleagues in theology exceptionally well, I cultivated a close relationship with the professors of German, music, Latin, and Russian. I also had a good and friendly relation with the professors of Spanish, history, and English. In those days most medium-size departments had only one professor, who was head of department. It is quite different nowadays, when there might be three, four, or five professors in the subject-area. They would have been promoted from senior lectureships or readerships within the department. This process has now reached such a pitch that fellow professors sometimes ask me, "Were you the *real* professor of theology, then?" In those days the vice-chancellor invited us every year to a residential conference together at a good, four-star hotel, and we became firmer friends, even across faculties.

It is easy to demonstrate that our staff collegiality in theology was often hilarious by the fact that our secretary would sometimes knock hard on the door of the staff coffee room to remind us that some students were taking exams, and will we please keep our laughter down to a reasonable volume. Our Welsh colleague, Dr. (later, professor) Douglas Davies would typically exclaim, "Well, got to laugh, haven't you?" I don't think that his ready laughter had anything to do with his academic specialisms, which included death studies and Mormonism. Indeed Douglas managed to acquire research assistants and grants in these disciplines, which at first favoured the department. The downside appeared later when an annual debt re-appeared regularly on the departmental accounts, for which the explanation was Douglas's comment, "I'm afraid that I forgot the Value-Added Tax!"

The staff in the department showed great trust. For in those days the head of department entirely ran the accounts and expenditure. Indeed, by taking responsibility for external students and degrees from the theological colleges of St. John's and Lincoln, we were able to amass some surplus. Since oversight of this work for the colleges had involved a lot of work, we felt that we were entitled to pay for a free lunch or dinner for the staff from time to time. This lasted until an anonymous lecturer in the Classics Department split on us, and the university authorities made it clear that we were not at liberty to purchase free meals for ourselves on this basis. As professor of theology, I was an ex officio member of the Councils of St. John's College, Lincoln Theological College, and the East Midlands Training Course. The three together took quite a chunk of time.

Initially our teaching staff numbered seven. We did so well with numbers of undergraduates and especially postgraduates that within a year or two our numbers were raised to eight and eventually to nine. We looked to appoint someone in Reformation and Historical Theology, and we appointed Carl Truman. Dr. Mary Charles Murray (alias Sister Charles) became a reader, and in due course Douglas Davies, a professor. I shared some supervision of PhD students with Philosophy, Linguistics, Critical Theory, and Education. Doctoral students came from England, America, Korea, Singapore, Taiwan, Romania, Australia, and all parts of the world. I inherited David Hilborn, now principal of St. John's College, who was quickly followed by several Americans, Mark Chan from Singapore, and many others. Dr. Lin, from Taiwan, already held a Tübingen doctorate from Moltmann.

Elections were held in due course for the Space Allocation Committee. This was chaired by a pro-vice-chancellor, with academic representation from the Arts and Social Sciences; the Sciences and Engineering; and the Faculty of Medicine. The other members were the bursar, the director of estates, and a lay member of Council. My personal concern was not only for good university planning, but also to keep theology in the splendid and convenient Trent Building. Thomas Wiedemann, professor of Latin, shared with me the problem of noise in his study, and asked me if I would ask for sound-proofing. It would cost £5,000. I proposed this, and it was passed, and in the next agenda item it transpired that if we invested £250,000 in the Engineering Building, Rolls Royce would add another half a million pounds. I need not have felt trepidation for asking for £5,000! Theology stayed in the Trent Building until I had to retire. It was also a good group for networking.

I also found myself on the Purchasing Committee. Once again, it had a similar representation, with the director of purchasing as chairman. One or two colleagues asked what might concern Arts beyond paper clips, but again, the networking and knowledge of management made this very worth well. I was astonished when I was described as a very useful member of the group. I hope that "useful" did not mean "uncritical."

Part of my job was to recommend names for the prestigious Firth Lectures to the vice-chancellor. Before I arrived my predecessor, Professor Heywood-Thomas, had suggested Elizabeth Schüssler Fiorenza, who would not have been my personal choice. We began with a very large audience in the Great Hall; the second lecture was much reduced in numbers; the third was a random scattering of stalwart feminists. I was not surprised. She spent time explaining that she would have held a more impressive post if she had not been a woman. The professor of history asked me, "What has any of this to do with theology?"

We were a department of all-male teaching staff except for Dr. Mary Murray. Evidently Dr. Schüssler Fiorenza regarded me as beyond redemption, for she aggressively grilled Dr. Murray about why our staff did not appoint more women, and why her audience was so very thin. I vividly remember Mary Murray's quiet reply: "This is not America, you know." I could not help comparing her audiences with my memory of Bishop Stephen Neil delivering three public lectures at the University of Bristol. The first lecture was well attended; the second, better; by the third lecture there was standing room only! In later years, for example in May 1998, I was able to invite Professor Pannenberg to give an outstanding series of the Firth Lectures, as well as others.

One special highlight was to be invited by the minister of health to serve on the Human Fertilization and Embryology Authority (HFEA). I suspect that Sir Colin may have suggested my name. Ruth Deech, principal of St. Anne's College, Oxford, was an excellent chairperson. We met regularly for HFEA meetings in London, but the entertaining events were regular inspections on site, which members of the HFEA were expected to chair. We had a team of geneticists, medics, and others to accompany us—probably about five or six in all. We scrutinized staff c.v.s; facilities for freezing; the secure storage of confidential files; and so on. The only problem was that any misdemeanour involved either withdrawing the licence ("an atomic bomb"), or a slap on the wrist, with "Don't do it again!" I imagine that I was the only inspector who had no science "O" levels.

Over several years I attended a number of HFEA conferences, which were open to clinicians and owners or managers of clinics. I overheard one clinician complaining to another about "all these Government rules and inspections." To which his companion replied, "Oh! You will soon discover ways of getting round those!" I was not surprised when it was suggested that spot inspections without prior warning should be put into place. The HFEA had multiple meetings in London. These included the Annual Conference; inspections of clinics in various locations; licensing committees (some for research licenses, others for treatment licences); the Research Committee; and the Ethics Committee; all over and above the regular monthly Authority meetings.

The Nottingham chair allowed me to go to numerous professional conferences overseas. Americans tend to regard the Society of Biblical Literature and American Academy of Religion joint conference as an expected attendance for which their universities or seminaries paid. Most conferences had 7,000–9,000 participants, compared with about 150 at the British Society for the Study of Theology. British institutions were less generous, but Nottingham University usually covered my expenses if I was giving a paper. They took over several good hotels. My first of many was at San Francisco in November 1992. I recall planning to see the harbour, and finding myself on a public tram full of British scholars. James Dunn and Tom Wright were certainly among them. As we arrived at our destination, the black tram conductor called out, "Keep the faith, man!"

In addition to supervising numerous PhD candidates, I taught hermeneutics as a third-year option, initially with only eight students. We bonded into a real friendship, and I can still remember their names. We entertained them at home for tea, but I no longer had time to repeat the regular Sunday teas of Sheffield days. On the last day of lecture-seminars, one of the eight brought a bottle of champaign for us. Nowadays it seems a fairly gruelling schedule: *two two-hour* lectures each week for a year (although less gruelling by American standards). But this was the same amount as the compulsory course on God, Freedom, and Evil, which was also obligatory for those philosophy students who had opted for joint-honours with theology. My course in Nineteenth-Century Theology also took two-hour lectures, but in the second semester this became Twentieth-Century Theology.

The rule for supervising students for the PhD or MPhil was that we gave a minimum of three supervisions per term of at least an hour; but I notice from records that it was frequently more. In April 1993, I received an invitation from Wheaton College, Illinois, to give two lectures on hermeneutics primarily to their faculty. I discovered that the Biblical Studies Department believed in literal exegetical meaning; the Literary Theory Department believed in a looser approach, often some version of Reader-Response Theory; and the Department of Philosophy held a balance, which was congenial to me!

Naturally I was approached to take on external examining. Exeter University invited me to examine Plymouth. Rather daringly, I agreed, provided that they could accommodate me in a good hotel on the sea front. This they kindly did for three years, with a splendid hotel on Plymouth Hoe. Examining PhDs was more frequent. One feels obliged to agree, since one needs someone else to reciprocate by examining one's own PhD candidates. So I went to Aberdeen, Birmingham, Cambridge, Durham, Edinburgh, and elsewhere. Sometimes it is difficult to say "no" to friends.

Everyone agrees that the fee for examining is what a Durham colleague called "derisory." Professor David Ford told me that he has to limit his to two each year, so I made sure to book him well in advance! Before his death, I regularly invited Professor F. F. Bruce to serve as external examiner. He disapproved of PhDs as an "American import." He viewed the British way as waiting for a DD in middle life. So he could be unexpectedly generous or lenient for PhDs. Those candidates whom he examined would usually exclaim to me: "Oh thank you; what a privilege to have Professor F. F. Bruce." I never told them that he was on my list mainly for weaker candidates who needed a generous examiner!

UCCA or UCAS interviews could be fun or tedious depending on whom one interviewed. I was always gratified that no student dropped out from our department while I was in post. Registering students for degree courses was the same. Most entertainment came from colleagues. One year I found myself seated between Philosophy and Sociology. A representative of the former whispered to me: "We hate Sociology; they imagine that logic and reason are wholly determined by birth, class, and environment!" A little later the man from Sociology whispered to me, "We hate Philosophy; they take no account of such vital factors as birth, class, and environment!"

Somehow I found time to lecture at several British universities as well as American ones. Dr. (later professor) Iain Torrance, editor of the *Scottish Journal of Theology*, and now Pro-Chancellor of Aberdeen University, invited me to deliver a series of four lectures in the University of Aberdeen. These were expanded into the book *Interpreting God and the Postmodern Self* (T. & T. Clark, 1995). That year I also changed and developed several courses. God, Freedom, and Evil, was divided into two parts: the first delivered by me; the second by Roger Gallie, lecturer in philosophy. The course in Nineteenth-Century Theology gave way to Creative Eras and Thinkers in Theology. Other adjustments were made, and my doctoral supervision rocketed as the number of PhD students increased. I was caught up in many meetings in London: the Association of University Teachers in Theology and Religious Studies (AUDITORS); in November 1995, my first General Synod, which would continue for fifteen years; the HEFA; the Doctrine Commission (for twenty-eight years); and many others.

We received many visitors from abroad: Maria Poutrova from Belarus; Nick Wolterstorff from America; Wolfhart Pannenberg and Jürgen Moltmann from Germany, and a number of others; and some from Britain, such as Professor David Ford. Conversely, I visited North Park, Chicago, and for the second time, Fuller Theological Seminary, Pasadena, California. Our department went on expanding: we appointed Seth Kunin, and if we included temporary teaching staff and special lecturers we had reached twelve. The bishop of Leicester was now Bishop Tom Butler, who received complaints from more traditional churches about the impact of Don Cupitt's "Sea of Faith" network on the Diocese. He therefore began a "Theological Issues Group," which met regularly, and of which I was a participant, to thrash out some of the issues. Some of the older clergy had clearly lost their faith, and were unresponsive, but most of the younger clergy were open to rethink their theology.

Far more important than overseas and British visits to other universities, more important than even examining and theological societies, was my personal research. The university had made it clear that an important duty of a professor was to provide a lead in the subject, not least in publications. "Research ratings," which influenced the prestige and finances of the university, played only a small part in this, because to my mind research was part of a theological calling anyway. In personal terms, the year 2,000 was a crucial one. I had worked for much of my life on 1 Corinthians. In the years running up to 2,000 I worked intensively on a commentary on the Greek text of 1 Corinthians. All in all, including indices and bibliographies, when Eerdmans published it, the book reached 1,446 pages + xxxiii. I presented a copy to the vice-chancellor. Normally an austere man, he confessed himself "tickled," and I am sure that it helped our department's research ratings. These were taken every four years, and I asked Mr. Jon Pott, vice-president of Eerdmans, to try to bring the book out in good time for the ratings.

I could never have achieved this without the constant practical support of my wife, Rosemary. She read endless pages to check typographical inaccuracies. In the end, she produced a virtually flawless draft which my secretary Janet Longley had typed. She typed in the Greek letters and words, which was a often a strain for someone who did not know Greek! At the same time, Rosemary drove me every day to the university. The reviews seemed amazing! Craig Blomberg, himself a writer on 1 Corinthians, wrote, "One of the most detailed, widely ranging, and exegetically compelling commentaries ever written on any book of the Bible!" *Theological Studies* wrote: "The exegesis is careful. . . . The volume is extremely lucid . . . and will serve the field of New Testament studies for many years to come!" It was published in the prestigious series New International Greek Testament Commentary in hardback, and, to my knowledge, is today the first of the series to be reprinted in paperback.

Over my ten years as head of department, I was able to deliver lectures in California (three times); Chicago (several institutions); Vancouver; Toronto; Boston; Utrecht, the Netherlands; Romania; Natal, South Africa; and Singapore. Singapore was among the most memorable. I visited there in 1999. When my taxi arrived at my hotel, a long line of porters was ready to collect by bags; another long line awaited me in the hotel; a battery of waiters attended my table. My host merely had to click his fingers, for another long line of waiters to appear. Oriental hospitality is remarkable. Hospitality in Korea was no less impressive, as the next chapter demonstrates. In Singapore I saw meticulously clean streets; fine botanical gardens; a hotel reminiscent of the imperial era; "holy men" walking on burning coals; and a Chinese historical museum. The cost of Mark Chan's small flat was astronomical. A Christian government official explained cultural differences from the West, including the tendency of adult children to stay living with their parents for many years. I lectured there to a large audience on postmodernism.

The visit to Oradia in Western Romania was also memorable. I travelled via Budapest, Hungary, with ancient buildings on both sides of the Danube. We drove to Oradia through Romanian villages, and I gave lectures in the university. The students were eager, but I could not help comparing their meagre library resources with those available in Britain and especially America. I could not fault Dr. Adonis Vidu, my brilliant Romanian doctoral graduate, for moving to Boston, America, largely on the ground of needing resources for research.

In 1998 the University of Nottingham re-organized many of its structures. 1997 was, I think, the last time that we held residential conferences for all heads of departments. In the face of many protests, the university lumped together a number of departments into "schools." The Arts professors insisted on retaining their departmental names. Professor Robert Pascal, professor of music, resigned. I suspect that since the introduction of research ratings, it may have been thought that departments were too cosy an environment for strict discipline to be shown to senior colleagues by heads of departments. Archaeology, Classics, Music, Philosophy, and Theology became the School of Humanities (though one wit suggested the School of Venerable Studies). History, American Studies, and English were somehow allowed to constitute their own school.

1998–2000 also witnessed the great honour of my being elected as the president of the Society for the Study of Theology, which I had attended since 1968. I was preceded by Professor David Ford, Regius Professor at Cambridge, and followed by Professor David Fergusson, professor of divinity at Edinburgh. By now the Society welcomed members from the Netherlands, Germany, Norway, and elsewhere, as well as British members, and we reached about 150 at our annual conference.

I gave my notice of retirement from the university two years before the due date of retirement, and this led to an appointment as professor and head of department with a period of overlap. Although one is strictly unable to serve on an appointment committee of one's successor, the appointee was not, equally strictly, my successor. So I was able to give a personal invitation to apply to Dr. Alan Ford, whom I knew from Durham days to be loved by students, and would be a superb head of department. In the event, he was duly appointed, and since that time has been first dean of Arts, and currently pro-vice-chancellor.

Life goes on in a generally happy, ambitious, and fulfilled university. I took my first "retirement" when I was sixty-five, because this was stipulated in my contract. Professor Alan Ford arranged a great "Farewell" for me at the end. Later on, as I recount in the next chapter, I was able to return to Nottingham in what was my fifth year as professor of Christian theology at Chester. It has always been a happy place for me.

As public orator on behalf of Nottingham University I read the oration for several honorary degrees. These included the archbishop of York, Most Revd. John Sentamu, pictured here with the vice-chancellor.

I gather that shortly after my retirement, two events followed. First, our department moved from the Trent Building after, I believe, some fifty years. The university needed more room there for Finance and Administration. Second, New Testament Greek ceased to remain a compulsory subject for single honours students. I am sure that many were relieved. Nevertheless, the problem arose that some of those who later wanted to specialize in biblical studies found that in effect this route was now blocked to them. But it was now a national trend. It was some years since Mark Noll, the American church historian, had expressed envy at the undergraduate training of British students on the basis of their biblical and linguistic training! I had always hoped that students could say to themselves about obligatory Greek: "If he or she can do it, I certainly can!"

1992–2002

Award of second DD by the Most Rev. archbishop of Canterbury, George Carey for published work in New Testament. This award-granting authority is given to archbishops of Canterbury, dating from the time of Henry VIII, in place of those awarded by the pope in earlier years.

Chapter 8

1995–2010
Theological Contributions to the General Synod

THE CHURCH OF ENGLAND General Synod is often grandly called "The Parliament of the Church of England." In many ways it has sought to model itself on the House of Commons, even down to electing approximately 575 members, plus a number of officers, passing regular resolutions or motions, with divisions, debates, reports, and numerous committees and subcommittees. When a member wishes to speak, he or she must stand and catch the eye of the chairman, who acts like the Speaker of the House of Commons. He or she may call or fail to call any one of a crowd who usually stand in the hope of speaking.

Like the House of Commons, the Synod may seem like a cosy club or network of friends on some occasions; while at other times it may seem to be characterized by unruly hostility, petulance, and high emotions. Synod is divided into three "houses": the House of Bishops, the House of Clergy, and the House of Laity. On occasion, a motion may be carried only by the agreement of all three houses. Each member of the Synod represents a particular diocese, although members are elected as individuals and not simply as a representative of the diocese. On average, each diocese will be represented by its diocesan bishop, together with about five clergy and about five or six laity. The larger dioceses will have a higher number of clergy and laity; the smaller dioceses will have less.

In addition to the election through the diocese, there are three or more "special constituencies." For example, the combined universities together elect six; some are elected from religious houses; some are suffragan bishops; and some are chaplains to the armed services. In the university constituency, Oxford, Cambridge, London, and Durham and Newcastle, elect one each. One is elected from the other southern universities, and one from the other northern universities. During my years of university teaching I had long hoped to stand for election to General Synod, but in earlier years Barnabas Lindars, professor of theology at Manchester, and James Atkinson, professor of biblical studies at Sheffield, had stood for the northern universities, and both were friends against whom I did not wish to compete. But in 1995, when I was professor of Christian theology at Nottingham, there was no such obstacle, and I stood for election with a statement about myself and my beliefs, and was duly elected in 1995.

The Doctrine Commission Report

In those days we met three times a year, in September, February, and July, although later the February meeting was discontinued. In my first two meetings of Synod, I often stood, but was never called to speak. My moment came in July, when the Doctrine Commission Report was debated in July 1996 in York. The difference of atmosphere between Westminster and York cannot be exaggerated. Differences in dress-code exemplified this. In London most men wore dark suits (at least in the 1990s). In York in summer they wore white jackets and open-neck shirts. I had been a member of the Doctrine Commission from 1975 to 2005, with a very short break. The Church of Scotland ecumenical representative, the Reverend Andrew Scobie, first praised the theological seriousness and sound hermeneutics of the Doctrine Commission Report, but then slated it for communicating in a solely "in-house" way, rather than making theology intelligible to the rest of the world.

Here came my chance! Fortunately I happened to know the chairman, and this time, when I stood, I was called to speak. I explained that when I boarded the train to York from home, I thought that I had two hours of train journey to re-read the report. But when I came to my seat, the three twenty-plus young men at the table first had to clear away about thirty empty lager tins to make room, and then they all saw me open the report, called *The Mystery of Salvation*.

I shortly received a dig in the ribs. "Oi, mate," one of them exclaimed, "Woss all this *Meest'ry of Sa'vation* stuff then?" (In my oral speech I was able to simulate his appropriately inebriated South London pronunciation or dialect.) I explained that it was a report on Christian doctrine, which included God, evil, salvation, heaven, and hell. In fact, we began a two-hour seminar on these themes. The seminar was virtually non-stop for two hours, except for dashes up the corridor in one direction to retrieve logarithmic increases in lager tins, and urgent rushes down the opposite corridor to deal with hydrostatic or hydrodynamic imbalances that resulted. As we passed the crooked and twisted spire at Chesterfield, one of them remarked, "Gor! I didn't think I'd drunk that much!" (I had originally used "hydrostatic," but was later corrected by another member of Synod to the effect that "hydrodynamic" would have been more accurate).

As we approached York one of them asked me, "Are you going to speak on this?" I replied, "I do represent the northern universities, and hope to explain some theological themes, but I have already attended two sessions and stood on my feet about twenty times, but have never been called to speak." One of the young men replied,, "Aw, mate! That's easy-peasy. Yoo just stand up where ev'rybody can *zee* you, and when ev'rybody's lookin' at yoo, *yoo just take off all yor cloze*." At this point in the speech I took my jacket off, and made as if to take off more of my clothes. A number of people afterwards commented that at this point tears of laughter were running down the cheeks of the two archbishops.

I finally returned to what the previous speaker had said when he criticized us for lack of communication to the world! I pointed out that our job as a commission was largely a wholesale one, after which we expected church members to retail the project in the way that I had managed to do on the train journey. I recounted Archbishop Robert Runcie's vision of what a doctrine commission should be, and argued that under the chairmanship of the bishop of Newcastle this was precisely what the Doctrine Commission had achieved. I expounded several of the themes. In the end I was able to propose an amendment to the effect that the Doctrine Commission Report deserved study on the part of every church person, together with an attempt to disseminate it more widely. The amendment was carried.

The Creed

My next significant contribution came in March 2000. I had had reservations about the English Language Liturgical Commission (ELLC) on the Creed in 1998, but in July 1999, the Synod seemed to take the views of readers and users more seriously. There was deep concern from grassroots members about using the very same phrase for the birth of Jesus through the agency of the Holy Spirit and the Virgin Mary as the human mother, virtually as if to imply that they were equal partners. On the basis of New Testament Greek and patristic scholarship, I supported an amendment which used the phrase "born from the Holy Spirit" (*gennasthai ek pneumatos hagiou*). This matched the use of "*ek*" in John 3:5–8 and 1 Corinthians 7: 7 (*charisma ek theou*).

This was what General Synod ought to be about. In my speech, I attacked appeals to the *Greek Lexicon* by Liddell, Scott, and Jones, on the ground that this primarily concerned classical Greek, and pleaded for more note to be taken of the Greek Lexicon of Bauer, Arndt, Gingrich, and Danker, and especially of Lampe's *Patristic Greek Lexicon*. I also cited the verdicts of Moulton and Milligan on the Greek papyri, and a number of patristic scholars, including Kelly. I used quotations from Athanasius and Basil of Caesarea for their use of *ek* or *from* in this context, and its value in resisting some mythological understanding of the Virgin Birth.

My speech was supported by the bishop of Rochester, Rt. Revd. Nazir-Ali, and the bishop of Liverpool, Rt. Revd. James Jones. The bishop of Rochester emphasized the correct defence of the wording against mythological interpretation of the Virgin Birth. In the end, when the resolution was put to the Synod, the ELLC version was defeated, and my motion was carried by thirty-eight bishops to zero; 197 clergy to twelve; and 149 laity to fifty-six. This was one of the most explicitly theological debates of General Synod ever. Some complained that we had spent a day simply on the preposition *ek*.

A Time to Heal

I had another opportunity to introduce some theology when the report on healing was debated in July. The Rt. Revd. John Perry, bishop of Chelmsford, introduced the report. It was called *A Time to Heal: A Contribution towards the Ministry of Healing* (Church House Publishing, 2000). The Panel included John Gunstone, Bishop Dominic Walker, and some ten others.

The report began by tracing a recovery of the ministry of healing during the twentieth century, including sacramental healing and prayer. Jesus, the report said, "Treated sickness and sin as different expressions of the one supreme evil in humanity" (p. 19). The report did not explicitly link this with the kingdom of God, although arguably healing was possible because the kingdom had dawned. The report stated, "In Jesus we see the complete and perfect functioning of spiritual gifts" (p. 32). The panel lamented "the general failure of the Church of England to respond to the gospel imperative to heal the sick" (p. 47). Some colleges and courses, they said, provided no training in this area. They gave bishops responsibility for urging the "scriptural importance" of this ministry.

The report advocated sharing with professionals in this ministry, and proceeded to discuss exorcism. Matthew 10:1 was seen as a commission to perform this ministry (p. 171). They did, however, recognize that theological controversy beset the subject, and that it invited the danger of abuse and manipulation. A "review group" should set up guidelines (p. 207). In the parish, they concluded "The healing ministry should be clearly defined as part of the Church's mission and ministry" (p. 280).

The Synod, as with many motions, regarded this understandably as motherhood and apple pie. You could hardly vote against it. When I was called to speak, I dutifully rehearsed some of its many helpful insights. But two things disturbed me. I well remembered Bishop David Jenkins of Durham observing that the higher were the expectations of healing, the more bitter the disillusion when healing seemed not to be granted. In my parish church this very event had occurred. Second, after praising its good things and hard work, I asked how any report on healing could fail to address the problem of those who had believed in faith, but had apparently received no healing.

I first illustrated the point from my parish. One or two had given joyous testimonies to healing. But for a grandmother in our congregation whose grandchild had died of a brain tumour, in spite of ceaseless prayer and trust, such testimonies were like rubbing salt into her wound. If healing was really a gospel *imperative*, how could this be?

I suggested that there were two ways forward. One was to teach the biblical lesson that in so far as the kingdom of God and the new creation *had arrived*, as it did in Jesus, unexpected healing events *may indeed occur* as signs of the *kingdom*. But the kingdom of God is now only *in process of dawning* in the *church*, and these signs therefore cannot be "expected." Sometimes God chooses to heal, but at other times he allows the normal processes of the natural world to continue. As Cullmann and many others have taught, we are still subject to *two sets of forces* until the kingdom of God has wholly arrived. The word *imperative* surely risks implying trying to force God's hand.

The second way forward is to survey the various responses of the biblical writings and of Christians down the centuries to the problem of pain and suffering. Paul had to accept his thorn in the flesh, and many early Christians were ill and died. Job had to accept his afflictions. Many, including Luther, have argued that faith can grow strong only when it has to encounter difficulties and disappointments. Why has not the report painted a two-sided picture more realistically?

There were rumblings of "here, here," among the members, and later a lay medic, Dr. Peter May of Winchester, made some similar points. Yet in his reply, the bishop of Chelmsford replied to my points about pain and suffering, "Such a task properly belongs to the Doctrine Commission, and is beyond the scope of this body." To me, this merely confirmed that the panel lacked some further badly-needed theological expertise.

The Crown Nominations Commission

The topic of the Crown Nominations Commission arose in November 2002. I had been elected as a "central" member of the Crown Nominations Commission for ten years. In my speech I reported that I was deeply impressed and satisfied by the conduct of this commission. The Synod had expressed the wish to raise the number of diocesan members from six to eight. I wanted to argue in my speech against this proposal. First, the diocesan members already held sway beyond their numbers. Whereas the "central" members carefully observed the advice not to lobby in like-minded groups, the diocesan members would frequently confer together, and present a united front about their likes or dislikes for a candidate. Second, the chairman always took great pains to ensure that the diocesan view had been taken fully into account. Third, the commission had already reached sixteen (fourteen plus the two secretaries), and more than sixteen began to make genuine dialogue less easy. Fourth, the central members had already gathered experience and skill, and several of the names re-appeared for consideration. Fifth, a diocesan bishop has *a national role* as well as a diocesan one. Yet such was the widespread scepticism about the views of the diocese being "heard," that the motion was carried.

Theological Training

This subject came up once again in July 2003. I had for some years served on the Theological Training Committee, and before that served on the Theological Committee of the Council for Academic Awards. I was often appalled that the training programme was so often dictated by the finances available, although many would dispute this. I had also served as Examining Chaplain to the bishop of Leicester, and heard from almost every ordinand how their part-time lecturers or tutors were not nearly as helpful and well-informed as their full-time staff. I pressed the case for full-time training, ideally in residential colleges.

University Representation

The Church Publishing House published *Synodical Government in the Church of England: A Review*, under the chairmanship of Lord Bridge of Harwich, with Rt. Revd. Alan Chesters, bishop of Blackburn, as vice-chairman. Understandably it recommended that the membership of General Synod should be reduced from 575 to 390. This would allow easier debate and more participation.

The Review Group must have been born optimists. For how many turkeys would vote for Christmas dinner? Everyone began to calculate whether they might lose their seat. In the end, the House of Bishops remained the same: forty-four diocesans and six suffragans. But the Clergy were to be reduced to 154, and the laity to 175. I pointed out that those of us who held full-time commitments in the university could never participate in all the deanery meetings and opportunities for networking, which normally characterized clerical life in the parish. We would not be well known enough to collect more than a handful of votes.

The decisive speech, however, came from Christina Baxter, chair of the House of Laity. She has spent most of her life teaching in theological college, and it was therefore out of profound modesty that she argued to the Synod that if they relied only upon expertise from the theological colleges, the Synod would miss out on the more intense theological research carried out by the staff of the better universities. To my surprise and delight, the universities were allowed to continue to elect university members.

The Lord's Prayer

I simply cannot remember the time or year of our debate on the Lord's Prayer. All I can recall is the Rt. Revd. Peter Selby, bishop of Worcester, was passionately in favour of formalizing in our Common Worship, "Bring us not to the time of trial." I agreed that *trial* could be a proper translation of the Greek *peirasmos*. But so was *temptation*. In lexical terms the debate was fairly even, but inconclusive. I argued, however, in the Synod that (1) there was no evidence that Jesus was speaking of an eschatological trial; and (2) Luther was one of many who regarded temptation and struggle as necessary to growth in holiness, provided that it was not greater than could be resisted. I forget the further details of the debate. But I remember observing that only the arch-heretic Marcion and the bishop of Worcester had put forward a certain argument, to the delight of the Synod. The bishop's replied that next time he would ensure that he spoke *after* me, not *before* me.

Women Bishops

I did not take part in the furious but often ill-informed emotive debates about women bishops, but served on several committees that had considered this question. The most significant was the Rochester Committee, whose report was brought before the Synod in February 2005. It was presented by Bishop Nazir-Ali of Rochester. The problem of this report for many was that it was too scholarly and fair-minded. I don't think that we actually produced anything new, except perhaps the findings of Eldon Jay Epp's book, *Junia: The First Woman Apostle* (Fortress, 2005), which had recently appeared. Epp, a distinguished textual critic, had undertaken careful research on the name Junia in Romans 16, and demonstrated beyond reasonable doubt that it named a woman, and should *never* have been translated *Junias*. Bishop Nazir-Ali kindly gave me the credit for making this point in the report. Since so much of the argument against women bishops hinged on there being only male apostles, one might have hoped that this would be decisive. But, lo and behold! Another committee was to be entrusted to present the same issues to the Synod again. Since I left the Synod, I am glad to report that, under the presidency of Archbishop Justin Welby, a more positive way forward seems now to be taking place.

Chapter 9

2002–12

Chester University and a Second Period at Nottingham University

IN 2002 I CONTINUED my Church engagements. These included the Women in the Episcopate Group; a college inspection; the Crown Nominations Commission; lectures at Leicester Cathedral and Cambridge; the General Synod; and other British engagements. I also visited Boston, USA, for a hermeneutics consultation. From July 18th to August 4th I undertook another visit to Fuller Theological Seminary. Apart from lectures and seminars there, I went with Professor Colin Brown and Professor John Goldingay to the Hollywood Bowl Symphony Orchestra. By the summer of that year I had officially retired.

I lost my magnificent study in the university Trent building, and had to transport all my books home. We dry-proofed an outhouse a few yards from our back door, which accommodated half of my books. It took a very long time and much effort to sort some 8,000 books. Rosemary put my philosophy of religion books and hermeneutics into broadly alphabetical order. Except for commentaries, which I kept in a spare bedroom, I was surprised to see that both philosophy and hermeneutics took more space than New Testament. I classified systematic theology by separate doctrines. The section on linguistics was conflated with hermeneutics, and a somewhat smaller section emerged on ethics.

One of my close friends was Dr. Peter Forster, who had been Senior Tutor at St. John's Durham, and was a patristics scholar. While I began as a professor at Nottingham, he became, first, vicar of Beverly Minster, and then bishop of Chester. He kindly suggested to me that I might consider teaching at Chester College, where he was chairman of Council. At first I was concerned about travel-time from Nottingham, but he persuaded me to visit Chester for an "interview."

The "interview" was held in the College, and conducted by the principal, Dr. Tim Wheeler, Bishop Peter Forster, and Dr. Ruth Ackroyd, Head of the Department of Theology. They very kindly did not grill me, but concluded that I should be welcome if I would like to join them. I warmed enormously to their determination to implement the Founders' vision of a Christian College, which would soon apply for university status. In the event, I was appointed professor of Christian theology. I could teach a course after my own heart on Biblical Foundations, Christian Theology, and Christian Application Today. Dr. Ackroyd called it "Roots, Shoots, and Fruit." I would also supplement Dr. Robert Evans' teaching on the New Testament by teaching 1 Corinthians, teach a course on philosophy of religion, and share some PhD supervision. PhD seminars proved to be very creative, especially since a number of graduates did not really know how to engage in genuine research. My lectures were scheduled for Thursdays and Fridays, so I had to stay in Chester for only one night each week.

Chester College had provided me with overnight accommodation in their Gladstone Centre, but this meant carrying books and clothes to Chester and back every week. In May, therefore, I made an offer on a house, and we exchanged contracts on 8th July. It was 19 Hatherton Way, a quiet oasis in Northgate Village, just outside the city wall, and near to the college and Cathedral.

I found the experience of teaching at Chester very fulfilling. A number of the students were mature students from other professions; some were on the diocesan ordination course. I soon came to dismiss any pretentious thoughts about second-class universities. Ruth Ackroyd took infinite care and patience over weaker students, and all of them seemed very willing to learn. Questions in class were intelligent and relevant. The only misunderstanding which I can remember was my attempt to excuse a student from Liverpool for lateness. My comment, "Well, she does come from Liverpool" was meant to excuse her for a long journey, but was widely misunderstood as a piece of anti-Liverpool repartee!

Among my various invitations to preach, one came from St. Paul's Cathedral, London, and the other from Westminster Abbey. In addition to this, I visited Queen's University, Belfast to deliver public lectures, and spoke on the atonement at the Fourth National Evangelical Anglican

Congress at Blackpool (where my talk was paired with that of the archbishop of Sydney, presumably in case I was not sufficiently conservative). In November I flew to Atlanta, to give another paper at SBL.

In course of time the problem of research ratings came round, and it was somehow known that the Nottingham Theology Department had begun as "3," and accelerated to "5" and "5+" under my headship. I was therefore invited by the dean of Humanities of Chester and its research director to advise on subjects and submissions across the board. This proved interesting and enjoyable, although I had sometimes to advise against certain submissions, to the disappointment of the lecturer concerned. In the event, Chester did better than expected, and I was consulted further about documentation for the application to become a university. This also went well, and in March 2012 Chester University conferred on me the honorary degree of Doctor of Theology, in part-recognition of these services to the university.

The years 2004–5 were largely a repetition of these varied commitments, except for the consultation in Rome sponsored by the *Scripture and Hermeneutics Group,* originally founded by Professor Craig Bartholomew and me. Together (although with more work from him) we planned and executed an eight-volume *Scripture and Hermeneutics Series*, published in the first instance by Paternoster Press and Zondervan, Grand Rapids, with sponsorship from the Bible Society and Cheltenham and Gloucester College. They kindly dedicated volume 2, *After Pentecost*, to me, on my main retirement, "In recognition of his work in biblical hermeneutics." My work on the various volumes varied, but I participated in all the consultations. One of my most striking memories comes from the consultation on the Bible and political ethics, which was focused on the work of Professor Oliver O'Donovan, whom I had known from first meeting him in Toronto. About half of our group came from America, and about half were British. We nearly began a new war, when one of the American participants called us "citizens." Oliver expostulated with typical *gravitas*: "No! We in Britain are *not* citizens; we are *subjects*!" This led to what politicians call "a robust exchange of views."

The volume on which I worked the hardest as editor and contributor was the sixth, *Reading Luke* (published in 2005). On this occasion the other joint editors, Craig Bartholomew and Joel Green, were engaged in different projects. I wrote on Luke and hermeneutics, and attempted to introduce the essays of Professor Howard Marshall, Dr. David Wenham, Professor François Bovon, and more than a dozen others. In June 2005 we held our consultation in the Pontifical Biblical Institute in Rome. This was held in Rome partly to facilitate continuing Catholic participation. Jean Vanier and several cardinals participated.

Volume 7 of this series came out of our deliberations in Rome, and was entitled *Canon and Biblical Interpretation*. It focused largely on the work of Professor Brevard Childs and theological interpretation. In my introduction I discussed the controversial status of a "canonical" approach, and outlined the contributions of Childs to biblical studies, as well as introducing the fourteen or so other essays. Professor Frances Young had also joined us. One of my abiding memories is the everyday table-talk of the cardinals. Several Italian cardinals assured us that one certain truth was that spaghetti would be served for every meal. Another memory is the traffic jam that arose because of the visit of the Italian president to the newly-elected pope, who had planned to come to our consultation, but regretted that he was "a little busy at the moment."

I had travelled to Rome with my doctoral graduate Dr. Mark Chan from Singapore. He had produced an excellent thesis on Christology, published by Brill of Leiden. We did have time to visit many of the sites. The Catholic bookshops were invaluable to me, since I discovered a number of Pontifical Biblical Institute theses and books that were unfamiliar to me, and which I could bring home. Mark's capacity for taking photographs was prodigious, which was just as well, since the battery of my own camera became exhausted. I felt sorry for Archbishop Rowan Williams, who remarked at dinner during one CNC that although he had visited Rome many times, his packed schedule of many meetings meant that he had never had time to see the sights. We were able to include all that we had hoped.

On my return, the more routine cycle of public lectures, teaching, and writing awaited me. In December 2003 my grandson, Andrew, was born, followed by his sister, Lucy, in December 2005. Our youngest son, Martin, and his wife, Jackie, were the proud parents. This brought our grandchildren to six.

The year 2006, however, was far from being routine. At least three significant events occurred. First, in January the Anglican Communion sent me to South Africa, nominated by the Anglican Primates (senior archbishops) to participate in the group devoted to training Anglican clergy. It was formally called Theological Education for the Anglican Communion, and my section specifically concerned the requirements and training of Anglican bishops. This group was formally called the

Bishops' Target Group. We met in Johannesburg, and toured some of the shantytown slums, where Christian churches were working with those suffering from HIV. The conditions in which many lived were almost beyond description, often with no sewage other than a street running with water, with corrugated iron huts for their homes, and with virtually no facilities at all. In spite of this, some were immaculate inside. The church workers showed enormous courage, dedication, care, and love.

Visit on behalf of Primates and Church of England to Johannesburg, South Africa, in 2006, which included visiting nearby Shanty Towns

Shantytown near Johannesburg

Our group followed closely the admonitions and requirements of 1 Timothy 3:1–7 on the requirements for a bishop, stressing his need for a pastoral heart, the bishop's call to be a guardian of the faith, his personal holiness, his ability to teach, his love for God's people, and other biblical qualities. I became particularly friendly with the archbishop of Mauritius, the Most Reverend Ian Ernest, as well as with many others. I then travelled to Durban, partly on behalf of the Southwell Diocese, because we have a special link with Natal. I preached in Durban Cathedral. My visit was also partly on behalf of Nottingham University, in order to establish relations with Natal University at Pietermaritzburg, where I also delivered a paper on 1 Corinthians in recent research.

I also participated in some of the classes taught by Dr. Gerald West, whom I had known as a PhD candidate from Sheffield days. He was thoroughly committed to hermeneutics, including practical application and commitment to inter-racial understanding between black and white uses of the Bible. Once again, I was conducted through some of the grossly deprived areas by the diocesan link officer from Natal. He casually commented to me during one trip, "If we are carjacked for our money and documents, please do not resist; you are better off robbed than dead!" Even the pleasant, well-appointed, house, in which I stayed, was surrounded by security gates and barbed wire. I was immensely moved by the stark contrast between wealthy white community and white tourists and the largely deprived black community living immediately close by.

A second significant event occurred on 14th February, which was no less momentous for me personally. The vice-chancellor of Nottingham University, Sir Colin Campbell, invited me to lunch with him one-to-one. It was mainly a social occasion. Towards the end of lunch, he asked casually, "Why are you giving your research ratings to another university?" I replied, "There is no delicate way of answering this, other than to say that Chester pays me a salary, and you have to be paid to submit research ratings on behalf of a given university." His response was mind-blowing! "Well," he replied, "That would be no problem! If you would like to rejoin our teaching staff, just dictate your terms!" I would be free to supervise whomever I chose, and could even ask for a room and a secretary!

I jumped at the opportunity! Of course the bureaucrats were less enthusiastic, citing tax rules to limit the salary, and concerns about the "irregular" room and secretary. But with the vice-chancellor and the Department of Theology behind me, I succeeded with both. We appointed Mrs. Karen Woodward as my secretary, who typed my books until my second period at Nottingham officially ended. By the end of five years, I had advanced from seventy to seventy-five years old, and the vice-chancellor had retired. The Head of School saw me in 2012, and in spite of strong support from the Department of Theology and its students, he suggested that at seventy-five I had "had a good innings." After all, he concluded, "You wouldn't want me to make a middle-aged lecturer redundant, would you?" Ironically, research ratings would have more than eclipsed any part-time salary, but would perhaps not have balanced school accounts just then!

During the rest of the year 2006 several events followed, including flying to Asbury College, Kentucky, to give a series of lectures. Nearer to home, successful election to the Appointments Committee of the General Synod, and to their Board of Education followed. In August I spoke to the C. S. Lewis conference at Cambridge, on the Good, the True, and the Beautiful, at the invitation of Professor Hal Poe.

I had earlier met Hal Poe, a relative of Edgar Allan Poe, when I enjoyed a delightful three weeks at Union University, Jackson, Tennessee. The three weeks as "Scholar in Residence" had been a wonderful experience. A class at Union University in New Testament Studies were all eager to learn, and every student in the class appeared to own a copy of my commentary on the Greek text of 1 Corinthians. In England even clergy had complained in General Synod that they could not afford to buy it, and asked me to write a shorter commentary (which I duly did in 2006). In England only the current archbishop of Canterbury (then Most Rev. George Carey) and the archbishop of York (Most Rev. John Sentamu) had been two of the very few to read all 1474 pages! No doubt other clergy were "too busy!" The New Testament class at Union University asked the most intelligent questions about Greek grammar, Greek syntax, and the Greek text.

I later fielded questions from their faculty. Their very last question was: "What exactly does a canon theologian do?" I explained that this usually depended on the bishop, ranging from little to much. At Leicester I had regularly taken the lead role on "theological issues" and conducted ordination retreats; in Southwell, the bishop graciously let me write letters on theological matters, which he signed, with the wry comment, "They will know it was you!" I was also amazed that faculty and students offered me lifts by car from one university building to another, when the distance was little more than a few yards. A black church organist asked me to speak, simply because "I love your accent!" There is an almost endless store of happy memories, including boundless Southern hospitality from both students and faculty! Half a dozen students took me to a restaurant for "Chicken 'n Dumplings," and Professor George Guthrie invited me to his home. Another faculty member (I forget who) took me to see the famous railway train at Chattanooga.

In November I gave another research paper on the Holy Spirit at SBL in Philadelphia. The third major event of the year, however, was my invitation to visit Korea in May. From May 23rd to 26th I visited several theological seminaries in Seoul, from 26th to 28th I travelled to Taejeon, both to preach to an enormous congregation in their Pentecostal church, and to speak again at several theological seminaries. The husband of my doctoral graduate, Dr. Sarah Ahn, was senior pastor of a very large church, whose everyday occupation was that of an excellent tailor. Believe it or not, he arranged for fittings in the vestry, while the congregation was arriving or leaving, and eventually I was presented with a marvellous Korean-made three-piece suit! Sarah has recently published *Interpretation of Tongues and Prophecy in 1 Corinthians 12–14* (Deo, 2013), and has been appointed president of the Asia LIFE University.

In Korea with two Korean PhD graduates: Stephen Choi and Sarah Ahn

This was not the end of spectacular events. A major road boasted a banner strung between buildings, which proclaimed: "Welcome, Professor Thiselton!" Wherever I lectured, most of my books were on display, with a long queue of people waiting for me to sign their copies. I received a conducted tour of ancient buildings, the lovely countryside, which included terraced rice fields, a Buddhist Temple, and a couple of Korean and Chinese museums. I think that I spoke in seven theological seminaries, one of which presented me with a gift for Rosemary, who was in England. I was also taken to a Korean Theatre, and given Business Class Fares to and from Korea. The Hotels in Seoul and Taejeon welcomed me to a suite with generous displays of flowers. I tried not to compare all this with typical hospitality of overseas guests in England!

Visit to Seoul and Daejeon, Korea, Preaching in Daejeon Church, on platform with my PhD graduate, Dr. Sarah Ahn, beside as translator

In January 2007 Rosemary and I spent about ten days very near to ancient Corinth. I was utterly familiar with what we wanted to see there, having written a very detailed commentary on the Greek text of 1 Corinthians and a shorter pastoral commentary on the same book. (One piece of humour which circulated in universities and at the Synod was that only Thiselton could produce a "Shorter" commentary of 325 pages!) Rosemary and I visited all the sites, and I took back power-point slides of the best dozen. These included: the Peirene Fountains; Acrocorinth; the Lechaeum Road; the Babbius Monument; the Ersastus Pavement; and so on. We discovered the Erastus Pavement in an overgrown field outside the Corinth Museum. We also climbed nearly to the top of Acrocorinth, but thought that we ought to turn round because our time was running out. In the event "Greek time" proved to be indefinite, and we waited a further hour in the vehicle which was to take us back. The hotelier where we stayed claimed to be a fan of Manchester United, but this may have been an embellishment for tourists from England.

In July I enjoyed my seventieth birthday. To my mind, birthdays ought to be celebrated, but only God adds to the three score and ten, when they become special marks of God's goodness. Rosemary kept things very quiet through the morning. Then the door bell rang, and when I answered it, to my utter amazement our six closest friends from the days of my London curacy stood there fifty years later, from London, Kent, and Norfolk (for the record: Judith, Gillian, Valerie, Clive, Margaret, and Terry).

This aside, on our return to England the normal cycle of events took over: speaking to the clergy of the Diocese of Derby, to the Diocese of Winchester, and so on. A fourth major event, however, came in August 2007, and stood in stark contrast to the earlier happy events of 2006–7. I suffered a very serious, major, stroke, during which the hospital told Rosemary not to hope for my recovery. The family was on holiday in the far corners of England, and were hastily convened for a family goodbye. I still recall the most horrible nightmares, but whether these were due to the stroke or to drugs, I shall never know. I am told that it was once again due to prayer and providence, and partly through the ministrations of a junior doctor, that I survived. Even the secular surgery called me "The Miracle Man."

On the day before the stroke I experienced serious dizziness. It was severe enough to call the doctor. He dismissed it as a "dizzy spell," and prescribed anti-dizziness tablets. I awoke next morning very unwell, although I recall coming downstairs in my dressing gown, and trying to index the proofs of *The Hermeneutics of Doctrine*. I began to collapse, and when I could not talk or walk, with a characteristic lop-sided mouth, Rosemary at once called an ambulance.

Clearly Rosemary's very prompt action constituted part of an essential step to eventual recovery. The six weeks in the University Hospital was full of nightmares, hallucinations, and imagined hostility of patients. Very gradually I surfaced to discover many, many letters, cards, and notes from Christian friends. I am sure that I owe much to Rt. Revd. George Cassidy, then bishop of Southwell and Nottingham, for his prayers, and probably to his urgent messages to praying friends. He was at my bedside almost at once, certainly before the family arrived. He visited me and prayed with me four or five times thereafter. Cards and gifts included lovely bouquets of flowers from the bishop of Leicester,

Rt. Rev. Tim Stephens, and from the bishop of Rochester, Rt. Rev. Nazir-Ali, with assurances of prayer for full recovery. Rosemary had written or emailed at once asking for prayer, and this was a vital means of our passing through the crisis.

At the same time Rosemary emailed Jon Pott, vice-president of Eerdmans, to explain the situation. She told him that the *Hermeneutics of Doctrine* was as much on my mind as anything, especially the need to ensure that it was published in time for the next SBL meeting in America. Eerdmans took over the proof-reading and indexing, and it was published in November 2007, in time for SBL and the research ratings. The book was greeted with extravagant reviews. For example, Archbishop Rowan Williams very generously wrote, "Anthony Thiselton is undoubtedly one of the most sophisticated and creative minds in the whole of the Anglican Communion today. . . . *The Hermeneutics of Doctrine* is by any standard a major work." Meanwhile in hospital the physiotherapists seemed like a brutal enemy, but proved to be vital friends. Eventually I could go to hospital chapel in a wheel chair. The Minister of Cornerstone Free Church, Rev. Peter Lewis, was also diligent in prayer and visiting, as well as my vicar and friends from my church. My other memorable experience with a wheel chair was when Rosemary wheeled me out to the car to see my badly-missed little Cavalier King Charles dog!

Inevitably recovery took a long time, but cognitive powers seemed undiminished. Soon I risked the ire of medical bureaucrats by starting PhD supervision at home, especially for Matthew Malcolm, who had travelled from Western Australia to be my doctoral student. He not only graduated, but became Senior Lecturer at Perth Theological College, and later was joint-editor of my *Festschrift* with Professor Stanley Porter, president and dean of McMaster Divinity College, Canada, from Sheffield days. My poor secretary, Karen Woodward, must have wondered about her future, but in due course she soon began working on my next book. I was still finishing teaching at Chester, and Chester required a "fit to resume work" certificate. The medic seemed surprised that I was clearly enthusiastic to resume work; mostly, he said, it is the opposite way round.

The worst long-term effect was on my legs. I needed a stick (more aesthetically called a cane in America), and could not stand for more than twenty minutes. Chester provided me with a "high" chair for teaching; at Nottingham I could sit for smaller classes. Attenborough, my local church, was doubtless relieved to know that no sermon would exceed twenty minutes. There had been some concern about my ascending the pulpit steps, so someone anonymously presented a lectern to the church. Our vicar, Sue Hemsley-Halls, informed me that the lectern would prevent a heart-attack. I protested that my heart was sound. She replied: "Not yours; members of the congregation watching you!"

At Nottingham, to my delight, I taught Hermeneutics and Themes in Systematic Theology, and supervised several PhD candidates. Matthew Malcolm was excellent on 1 Corinthians, exegesis, and Greek. I had already supervised a Leicester priest, Rev. Mandy Ford, for the MPhil on Paul Ricoeur; now she was very well equipped to undertake research on his hermeneutics, narrative-theory, and work on tragedy, for the PhD. Andrew Talbert, from America, was well-informed on Thessalonians and Reception Theory, and later helped with indexing my books, and assisting Stanley Porter and Matt Malcolm in editing my *Festschrift*. I also taught hermeneutics for the MA. The year 2008 was fairly predictable, although enlivened by my being University Orator for the award of three or four honorary degrees. The most difficult of these from the point of humour was the Catholic bishop of Nottingham. I gathered that his one recreation was playing Irish tunes on the violin. So the best that I could do was to imagine the headline "Bishop on the Fiddle."

Humour was easier for most of the others. The archbishop of York, Most Rev. David Hope, was known to enjoy fast cars, whiskey, and arriving early at churches. He arrived in York after a very busy time as bishop of London. As he sank gratefully into his pillow on the first night, I am told, his peace was shattered by a tourist boat on the River Ouse just below his bedroom window, from which amplified sound blared out at full volume the song, "Money! Money! Money!" Such stories could easily be multiplied. His successor as archbishop was Most Revd. John Sentamu. Here lay humour in abundance. He had been made an honorary Yorkshireman, jumped from a plane or helicopter in a good cause, and was a limitless mine of fun.

At the end of one earlier oration, the professor of Latin, Professor Thomas Widemann, observed to me, "One joke is obligatory; two jokes are admirable; but three constitute a work of supererogation (he was a devout Catholic). This is possible only for an accomplished clergyman!" In 2009 my book *The Hermeneutics of Doctrine* was nominated for the Michael Ramsey Prize at the Hay Festival of Literature. It did not win, but it was great to be nominated among the first four, and to be part of the festival at which Archbishop Tutu was the main speaker.

The year 2010, however, brought two of the highest honours to date. I was elected a Fellow of the British Academy. Vice-chancellors had called this the highest accolade for a scholar in the Arts and Humanities. I attend their London meetings regularly. At the time there were about nineteen or twenty in theology, and more in other subjects. The second honour was to be chosen as a Fellow of King's College, London. This involved a splendid ceremony, in which degrees were also conferred. I recall sitting on the platform next to the dean of King's, Professor Richard Burridge, a friend from General Synod, who whispered, as the students filed past to receive their degrees: "It seems that the higher the class of degrees, the higher the mini-skirt!"

Award as Fellow of King's College (F.K.C.) in 2010, for distinction in scholarship

More routinely, I gave the Sarum Lectures on Wisdom, and another seminar at Oxford. But in January 2011 I received another high honour. I was awarded the Vice-Chancellor's Achievement Award at Nottingham. It was awarded partly for excellence in research, but mainly for building up the Department of Theology both in numbers and in national recognition.

2002-12

The University of Nottingham awards The Achievement Award both for distinction in research and scholarship and for building the reputation and numbers of the Department of Theology over the years

In April I spoke again at the Society for the Study of Theology at York, and in June conducted the wedding of my grandson, Jason. Jason wanted it to be a markedly "Christian" wedding. He was, however, concerned lest his wife's parents would regard this as over the top. In the event, they declared that they were most impressed. The same month we acquired Millie, our fourth Cavalier King Charles dog in thirty years. In September Rosemary and I took her to a dog training course, for which we were awarded a certificate which cast my four doctorates into the shade!

In October I participated in a consultation at the Royal Society International Centre, near Milton Keynes. This was sponsored by the Templeton Foundation. Two theologians met with a dozen or so neuroscientists, geneticists, and psychologists, to discuss the uniqueness of humankind in relation to animals. The resultant book was to be edited by Professor Malcolm Jeeves, and Eerdmans will publish it. In 2009 SPCK published my book *Paul: An Introduction*, which represented my first book after the stroke, and in the same year Eerdmans published my *Hermeneutics*.

The University of Chester awarded me the Honorary D'Theol decree in 2012 for scholarly distinction and for contributing to the recognition of Chester as a strong university

In 2011 Wiley-Blackwell published my commentary, *1 and 2 Thessalonians: Through the Centuries*. I gathered from fellow-contributors to the series that this was very hard work. In addition to New Testament exegesis of passages in Thessalonians, it took a huge amount of research to discover how these epistles were received over the centuries. In one sense the discipline of "reception history" was coming into fashion, and it had been tempting to publish with another mainline publisher. But with hindsight, it took an exceptional amount of work to produce one volume.

In 2012 two further pleasant honours came my way. First, I received the honorary degree of Doctor of Theology from Chester University, for services to that University. Chester always has impressive ceremonies in Chester Cathedral, and this was no exception. It was a fitting way of concluding the ten years that followed my formal retirement from Nottingham. I shall always be grateful for sharing in the growth and development of this Christian University. Second, my former doctoral graduates arranged for a *Festschrift* to be presented at a "Thiselton Conference" held in the University of Nottingham.

The Thiselton Conference was the occasion of the presentation of a Festschrift and several speeches of congratulation on a long and successful career in academia. Here my Singapore PhD graduate stands alongside Rosemary and me. The editors are from Canada (Prof. Stanley Porter) and Australia (Dr. Matthew Malcolm). Visitors came from various parts of the world

Two of them initiated, masterminded, and edited the volume. Professor Stanley Porter had become president, dean, and professor at McMaster Divinity School, Ontario, Canada. Dr. Matthew Malcolm is now Senior Lecturer of Trinity Theological College, Perth, Western Australia. Stanley Porter has many impressive publications in New Testament, linguistics, and hermeneutics. Matthew Malcolm has written excellent work on 1 Corinthians and Corinth. The Conference was held in June 2012, and Eerdmans published the *Festschrift, Horizons in Hermeneutics,* in 2013. In June 2012 I heard the original papers, and was given a preview of most of the essays. The essayists included both teaching colleagues: Professor John Goldingay, Professor James Dunn, Professor Richard Bell, and Professor Tom Greggs; and my doctoral graduates: Mark Chan, Richard Briggs, David Parris, Stephen Fowl, John Thomson, and the editors. In all, the volume exceeded 300 pages.

The Thiselton Conference was well attended and lively. Tributes of various kinds were paid, and Mrs. Anne Holt spoke movingly on behalf of the Bible Society. She urged that I had blazed the trail to making explicitly Christian scholarship and research "respectable." Richard Bell also spoke generously of my care for undergraduates. My daughter,

Linda, and grandson, Jason, were present to hear the speeches, and found them not only moving, but as explaining why I gave so much time to students, when I might have spent more time with the family. In early years I had spent much time with the family, constructing a dollhouse, a Wendy house, building snowmen, laying out model railway arrangements, and so on. But as head of department I had doubtless spent less time with the family than they might have expected, and the words of the speeches helped to put things into perspective on both sides.

A final blessing on the day of the Thiselton Conference came from Professor Jürgen Moltmann of Tübingen. I had long admired his work, read most of his books, and delivered the oration at his honorary Nottingham degree. He could not now travel from Tübingen, but sent a lovely, warm, personal message. He congratulated me precisely on the subject of this book: to be both a scholar and a churchman, mentioning especially my commentary on 1 Corinthians and other works. The day brought my time as formally a member of staff at Nottingham University to a fitting end.

Meanwhile a doctoral graduate from South Wales, Dr. Robert Knowles, had been studying my work and especially my hermeneutics for some time. His meticulous thoroughness was breathtaking. He had read everything that I had ever written, including early articles from the 1960s and 1970s in the *Church of England Newspaper*, the *Churchman*, and *Anvil*, which I had long since forgotten. I had written probably a hundred such articles, including research papers. Finally, after several revisions he published *Anthony C. Thiselton and the Grammar of Hermeneutics: The Search for a Unified Theory* (Paternoster, 2012, 672 pages). This surveyed the emergence of my hermeneutical theory from 1959 to 1970, a second developing period from 1970 to 1980, and a meticulous and detailed discussion of my book *The Two Horizons* (1980).

Dr. Knowles examined my interaction with epistemology (the theory of knowledge), tradition, language, and culture, together with my uses of Wittgenstein's philosophy and responsible biblical interpretation. He shows himself especially acute in confronting my critics, arguing rightly that these have too often simply misunderstood my work. His project is ongoing. He will next provide comparable analysis of my *New Horizons in Hermeneutics* (London: HarperCollins and Grand Rapids: Zondervan, 1992, and reprint 2012), which examines the hermeneutics of specific biblical texts and genres more closely than earlier work. In due course he hopes to work on *The Hermeneutics of Doctrine* (Eerdmans, 2007), and other more recent works. The value of his work is not only to view my work in broad chronological and inter-disciplinary terms, but also to take on board misunderstandings and criticisms which I have often not bothered to take up.

Three generations of Thiseltons

2012–14

Epilogue

When I finally left teaching students, at first I was devastated. The students and the Department of Theology unanimously wanted to continue having lectures on hermeneutics, and had asked for a further extension to my contract. It seemed as if I was leaving entirely so that the head of school could balance his account books. When we raised the issue of student demand, we were told that this was irrelevant. Emeritus professors are in a kind of limbo or no man's land. They have the status of members of Senate and may constitute admired models of research, but they are no longer members of the teaching staff, and usually lose both their room and secretary from the university. My old friend Professor Malcolm Jones felt this ambiguity keenly.

Yet in the end, the new-found freedom allowed much more time to write. I instantly finished writing *The Holy Spirit: In Biblical Teaching, through the Centuries, and Today* (Eerdmans and SPCK, 2013). This won the award for the best book on theology from *Christianity Today*, an American publication with a truly massive circulation.

A LIFETIME IN THE CHURCH AND THE UNIVERSITY

THE 2014 CHRISTIANITY TODAY BOOK AWARDS

We Recognize
EERDMANS
for

THE HOLY SPIRIT
by Anthony C. Thiselton

Award of Merit in the category of
Theology/Ethics

Mark Galli, Editor   CHRISTIANITY TODAY   Katelyn Beaty, Managing Editor

Out of the blue, *Christianity Today* certified my book on the Holy Spirit as the best book in theology for their 2014 Award

    I then worked on a large, single author, *Companion to Christian Theology*, which Eerdmans accepted for publication, and is due in 2014. I further fulfilled a long-held ambition to write and to complete a one-volume *Systematic Theology* (in the press, my twentieth book). I have recently received an invitation to participate in a consultation sponsored by the Templeton Foundation and the University of Aberdeen which will explore questions about life after death. The beauty of this for me was that this fourth book which I wrote after my stroke, namely, *The Last Things: A New Approach* (Eerdmans and SPCK, 2012), is to be taken as the main discussion book of the consultation. The archbishop of York, the Most Revd. John Sentamu, generously wrote, "Deeply grounded in Scripture, pastorally helpful. . . . What a real gem of a book!"

    In the event 2013 became a bumper year. First, it was the year of our Golden Wedding Anniversary, which we were able to celebrate, first with our three adult children and six grandchildren. Then, second, we held an open home for our local parish church.

Golden wedding celebrations in 2013

In 2014 I felt flat and rather depressed because for the first time for forty years I had no writing project before me which would bring good for the kingdom of God. In due course I began to write the first chapter of "recollections" of my life in the church and the university. I wanted to record how God had constantly, even miraculously (in spite of my reservations about this word), brought me through times of danger, poor eyesight, and dubious health, to succeed in writing, teaching, and, I hope, in church ministry. Moreover, since I had taught in five British universities and three theological colleges, as well as numerous seminaries or universities in some dozen countries, I proposed to write not an autobiography, but *A Lifetime in the Church and the University*. At first a sample MS was rejected, again, a first for me, on the ground that the new genre would constitute a publishing risk. Several friends joined me in prayer about what I should try to write. A number of my doctoral graduates, including several Americans, together with my friend Dr. Tim Hull, encouraged me to persevere with "Recollections." To my delight, Wipf and Stock, through their editor Robin Parry, expressed their willingness to publish this book.

Then on the very same day in June, Mr. Philip Law of SPCK emailed me to invite me to write *Discovering Romans*, to be published jointly with Eerdmans, and Mr. Jon Pott of Eerdmans emailed me to accept my proposal to write *Doubt, Faith, and Certainty* for them and probably SPCK. What an answer to prayer! I had up to three years work, which they would both allow me to write simultaneously, if I am spared to finish them.

As was the case in writing on 1 Corinthians and 1 and 2 Thessalonians, Rosemary wondered how I could hope to say anything genuinely new about Romans when so many had already worked on it as commentators, even in previous generations. The answer is easy. First, each new commentary assimilates what is best in the others, and seeks to build on this. Second, it is easy to find neglected areas. On Romans, I am convinced that Paul's struggle to write 1 Corinthians only three years earlier made a profound mark upon him, and suggested new ways of approaching (1) the priority of God's grace as the basis of everything; (2) the relation between Jewish Christians and Gentile Christians (or "the strong" and "the weak") in fragmented groups of Christians (where none can be "second-class citizens"); (3) the working out of God's promises in public history; (4) the implications of being "limbs" of Christ within Christ's one body; and (5) how Paul's impressive network of friends in chapter 16 gives the lie to his being caricatured as a misogynist! A commentary gives an opportunity to unravel both the historical and practical significance of all this, and shows how every chapter of Romans, and not just chapters 1–8 is important. The SPCK-Eerdmans series allows some work on reception history. In what ways did Romans change the lives of Luther, Wesley, and others?

The examination of faith, doubt, and certainty breaks down popular misconceptions no less. Doubt can sometimes be good, and at other times tragic. Some are too arrogant to admit any doubt, although doubt leads to self-criticism. Others seem to relish doubt, as if it seems to make them more human. But then why has God been pleased to give us revelation, rather than relying merely on purely rational discovery? The term *doubt* depends on the context of discussion. *Faith* is similar. The faith of justification means effectively appropriation of the work of Christ. But sometimes it is used in the Bible to mean obedience or confident trust. *Certainty* can be a deceptive circular journey of fabrication, as it was in Descartes' rationalism. But it can also become a gift from the Holy Spirit. A book allows the elaboration of such ideas.

The story goes on; but with preaching and officiating in my local church, and much writing, even if no formal university duties remain (except for occasional contacts there), there is much Christian work to be done. In practice, the job in the university is not exactly what it used to be. I have sympathy with my previous doctor, who took early retirement with the comment, "The job is no longer the work which I trained to do." University teachers and medics are both submerged today under a heavier bureaucracy than had characterized earlier years. Even ministry in the parish has changed. Sometimes secretaries and computers seem to have greater priority than curates!

One great advantage of the calling to be a Christian scholar and clergyman is that one can still write and still preach, even if, after the stroke, preaching has to be limited to a maximum of little more than fifteen minutes. Theological societies prevent simply a shrinking world becoming smaller, and the generous university superannuation allows a modest attendance at them. The British Academy keeps me abreast of both the subject and politico-educational events. Although the medics remain cautious about the effects of any long-haul flying, emails cost nothing, and many friends and colleagues are only an email away. I am not of the generation readily to use social media, but this is no cause for regret

Even ministry overseas is not beyond the scope of the writer. I vividly recall the sermon at my confirmation. The then bishop of Guildford preached on the text: "You will be my witnesses in Jerusalem, in all Judea and Samaria, and to the ends of the earth" (Acts 1:8). He stressed that for us Jerusalem represented our home; Judea was our country; and the ends of the earth represented the overseas mission field. Through most of my 'teens I struggled with whether God was calling me to overseas work. I gently tried the door of an overseas missionary society. Their response can easily be summarized: "With your health record, you must be joking! Continue to work towards ordination!" Looking back, I came to realize that my books reach overseas in great numbers, far more than I could have reached as an overseas missionary. Already five books have been translated into Korean, and one into Russian, while others are in process of being translated into Indonesian and Portuguese (for Brazil). The ways of God are wonderful, and often beyond human imagination, certainly of that teenager, long ago!

I am so grateful to God that I have written and completed eight more books after being rescued from this nearly fatal stroke in 2007. This involves at least two miracles. First, I had been told by a Harley Street medic that I could never read sufficient books to exercise a useful parish ministry; second, God had rescued me from a stroke that the medics expected would be fatal. This book has recounted many further acts of providence. It remains appropriate to end on the note of heartfelt thanksgiving to God and to all who have made it possible to live out this calling.

Anthony in his study, where over twenty books have been written